Inside Fatherhood

The Bible Reading Fellowship
15 The Chambers, Vineyard
Abingdon OX14 3FE
brf.org.uk

The Bible Reading Fellowship (BRF) is a Registered Charity (233280)

ISBN 978 0 85746 569 6
First published 2018
10 9 8 7 6 5 4 3 2 1 0
All rights reserved

Acknowledgements
Unless otherwise stated, scripture quotations are taken from The Holy Bible, New International Version (Anglicised edition) copyright © 1979, 1984, 2011 by Biblica. Used by permission of Hodder & Stoughton Publishers, an Hachette UK company. All rights reserved. 'NIV' is a registered trademark of Biblica. UK trademark number 1448790.

Scripture quotations marked MSG are taken from *THE MESSAGE*, copyright © 1993, 1994, 1995, 1996, 2000, 2001, 2002 by Eugene H. Peterson. Used by permission of NavPress. All rights reserved. Represented by Tyndale House Publishers, Inc.

Every effort has been made to trace and contact copyright owners for material used in this resource. We apologise for any inadvertent omissions or errors, and would ask those concerned to contact us so that full acknowledgement can be made in the future.

A catalogue record for this book is available from the British Library

Printed and bound by CPI Group (UK) Ltd, Croydon CR0 4YY

Inside
Fatherhood

Today's fathers tell their stories

David Atkinson

with reflections by
Mark Chester

For Maya and Olivia.

Because their dad loves them always.

Contents

Introduction

It is a wise father that knows his own child.
The Merchant of Venice II.ii

It is my birthday – my 40th year to heaven.

As I'm sat in the front seat of the car, the two girls tucked in safely behind, black sheets of rain are cascading down the windscreen. It sums up the day. I have come to buy the only birthday present I will receive today and ended up taking shelter in a car park in an out-of-town shopping area while the July weather rains down a thousand relentless blows.

I know my children, and they are fretting now. The windows are rapidly steaming up, each raindrop echoing like the approach of a distant giant. The mid-afternoon light has started to take on an eerily forbidding gloom.

It is, as we huddle here against the storm, just a couple of months since my mother died of cancer. Olivia is too little to understand it; Maya is still struggling to process it. For me, it's less than 60 days since the funeral. And I've been far too busy trying to be strong for everyone else to even consider how the events may have taken their toll on me. Besides, even if I had reflected upon it, what could I have done about it anyway? People needed me.

Time to think

That's what being a father means to me in this moment: being the cornerstone. It is a vision of fatherhood probably, in part, learned from my own father – yet somehow different. So many aspects of fatherhood have shifted in just one generation. It's no longer an evening-and-weekend job. It's no longer conducted from behind the sports pages of *The Daily Telegraph*. The demarcation has changed. So where do I fit in? Where do we all fit in now as men and fathers as the tectonic plates shift underfoot? It sets me pondering.

I am aware that Father's Day – that is, the annual appreciation of fatherhood not the high-street sales opportunity – will soon mark a major anniversary. Popular history suggests the Father's Day Council can be traced back to America in 1938, while US President Lyndon Johnson signed a proclamation for the third Sunday of June to be Father's Day in 1966.

With Father's Day turning 80 in 2018, it feels like a good time for fathers to reflect on their beliefs and values.

I am reflecting while parked in the biblical rain of a moribund July afternoon. There is no party this evening to get ready for, no cake cooling on a kitchen shelf. My mind is on other things anyway: I know my relationship with the girls' mother is over.

But that's not the difficult part. The greater dilemma strikes at something far deeper. Why should my relationship with my two beloved daughters suffer just because my life with their mother is at an end? After all, these two little girls have done nothing wrong.

Plenty of people would offer reasons in the months to come: the health worker who struggled to understand it; the solicitors who brought their preconceptions to the table; even a father of a girl in my daughter's class who assumed I'd be taking a back seat from now on. Children belong with their mother, right? I don't buy that. Is it so hard to understand that a man loves his children? Personally, I don't see divorce and fatherhood as mutually exclusive.

There are, of course, lots of terrible dads – they're well documented.

But there are also lots of devoted, caring fathers who make the sacrifices, sideline the selfishness of youth and take their responsibilities seriously. They have their failings and inadequacies but their motives are pure.

The point is that dads care too. But, they may ask in their darker moments, who cares for them?

I started to think about them and how their voices should be heard. There's a whole generation of dads away from the locker room and the pub snug with feelings and troubles and worries. They may be fallible, but they still love their children.

Seeking support

I knew in the months to come that I would need support. So I actively sought it out. A local Families Need Fathers (FNF: 'because both parents matter') support group put my situation in context; an old friend didn't falter with check-in calls; and another father would trade divorce Top Trumps with me in the car park after the school run.

Most of all, I became a regular at my local Who Let The Dads Out? group, and I joined a group of men following its Daddy Cool programme, both through a local church close to home. This framed the discussion around the experiences of others and grounded it in aspects of faith. The leader, Ben, ran both groups without judgements or comments. He simply encouraged the groups, all of us fathers struggling with our own set of different life circumstances, to share experiences and supportive advice.

We didn't reach many existential conclusions over pizza and bottled lager in Ben's front room during those November evenings. That didn't matter. But we did talk about our lives, explore feelings about being a father today, and raise questions about faith and morality that many of us had not even considered since being in Sunday school or the absent-minded bustle of the classroom. Most of all, we considered not just how we were looking out for each other, but also how someone was looking out for us all.

Five years on, I'm not keeping a watchful eye out for my name on the Queen's New Year's Honours list. I don't even expect many people really to empathise. I'm the only one who really knows the truth: my course was treacherous but I steered through the choppy waters with rational thought and both hands on the wheel.

I take peace these days from the fact that I stood at the crossroads, agonised about the different paths open to me and then made the best of my choice as I could see it. I looked within and above. I listened to the voice inside.

There have been sacrifices along the way, exhausted evenings and sleepless nights. There are, doubtless, more to come. Life is, I know, a constant journey, not a fragment frozen in zero gravity. Like many fathers, I've tried hard to maintain the strong relationship with my children. Like many, I too have tried hard to set a good example and demonstrate to them that, while life is sometimes difficult, some things are worth striving for. I've kept moving forward.

Moving on

I've seen other men moving forward too, as indeed are all the men I've had the privilege of sharing stories with for this book. As we move towards celebrations to mark 80 years of Father's Day, men live in fast-changing times. Male mental health is firmly on the agenda for discussion; male role models are more needed than ever before; and appreciation of the value of fathers is improving.

Dads, I venture, our stock is rising.

From writer-turned-FNF patron Louis de Bernières to footballer-turned-children's author Frank Lampard, high-profile figures are bringing the discussion about the changing nature of fatherhood into the mainstream. Most notably, Princes William and Harry have both spoken out recently about their lives in the context of mental health and fatherhood. Like all the ordinary, extraordinary talking heads in the chapters to follow, they have talked about how being a good dad is tough.

For example, Prince William told an Asian TV network in 2016 about his own experience of fatherhood. It's a story all father's share. 'There's wonderful highs and wonderful lows. But I've struggled at times,' he admitted. 'The alteration from being a single, independent man to going into marriage and then having children is life-changing.'

Like all fathers, I suspect, he's simply doing his best.

I always was. Back at the car park, the girls tucked in safely behind and the sheets of rain still lashing the windscreen, we are, at least, together. I go back home and see out the day in the knowledge that the next landmark birthday will be different. There is, despite all, some cake and it tastes good.

Storms will rage and subside, but I know my children. I know there's one simple truth for me as a father to two girls who deserved a loving dad: I was there for them.

Reflection

As I read David's story one word comes to mind: aloneness. It's not that David ever says he was alone – there were his daughters, his support group, Who Let The Dads Out?, his friends – but in his words I sense a feeling of isolation, if not physically then emotionally. He is buying his own birthday present, has lost his mother, is at the end of a relationship and is not being understood by the professionals he comes into contact with. He is busy being strong and has no space to process his own emotions.

Fatherhood, particularly at times of stress and change, can be a lonely business. We try to be strong, to keep our emotions hidden and adopt a steady, stoic manner in the face of loss, but beneath the surface we have a need. A need not to be alone, and with it a fear of being deserted. It is primal, this compulsion to want security in our relationships. Many childhood anxieties are fueled by the fear of being left alone.

We were created by our heavenly Father, God, to be in relationship with others, and as David has been created in God's image there is something deep within his spirit that knows his children need him and his constancy. Touchingly, he finishes his story with the words 'I was there for them.' It is a promise God has made to us too:

> Be strong and courageous. Do not be afraid or terrified... for the Lord your God goes with you; he will never leave you nor forsake you.
> DEUTERONOMY 31:6

By being there for his children, David is replicating God's model of fatherhood, and although he may not make the Queen's Honours list, I know God notices.

1

Stepdad – Dom

To overcome a disability and pursue a high-octane lifestyle in music are challenges enough for a young man. But then, one morning, he wakes up with a ready-made family unit and a sudden need to grow up. The secret? Keep smiling.

Dom laughs, 'I jumped straight from zero to 60.'

'Family life was gifted to me in a neat little present box,' he grins. 'One day I was hanging out with bands in the States. Next I moved into a terraced house with my partner, Stacey, her 13-year-old son, Xander, a dog and two cats.'

We're sat in a bustling city cafe, pouring the first of numerous pots of tea. Bearded hipsters in lumberjack shirts serve our tea on Scandi-chic wooden trays. But Dom is not fazed. Indeed, he breaks off from our conversation to greet the waiters as they pass, peppering the exchanges with nods and 'Yeah, cool man.' I get the feeling they quite like him using the cafe as an extension of his laptop-toting workspace.

'I still don't want my own children,' he tells me, sploshing milk into a sturdy, workman-like mug. 'I had done the good uncle thing but always thought, "Well, I can give them back afterwards."' He laughs again, and I can see why *The Independent on Sunday* voted him one of the happiest people in the country in 2013. 'Becoming a stepdad is the biggest decision I've ever made,' he adds. 'While my extracurricular music stuff keeps me balanced, the family is my life now.'

As we chat, Dom is waiting on the paperwork to become Xander's legal stepfather. The lad has a lot of anger, Dom explains, and was recently caught selling cigarettes to the younger kids at his school. Dom is heading home after our meeting to discuss with Stacey how to respond to the school. After that, he has a tour to plan, taking his hardcore punk band, Seep Away, out around the UK. Life is nothing if not interesting.

'Neither Stacey nor Xander have ever had a father figure. Xander has never met his dad and has no interest to do so,' says Dom, continuing with his open, ask-me-anything demeanour.

'It's simple,' he adds with a matter-of-fact air. 'You have to accept a lot of compromise when you get into a relationship with a single mum.'

The story so far

Dom arrives at our meeting with the look of Nirvana frontman Kurt Cobain, handling questions with shakes of his straggly, bottle-blonde hair and a touch of rock-star swagger. It's a far cry from his younger days as a wheelchair-based child with cerebral palsy in Beverley, East Yorkshire. He has had multiple operations on his legs and feet, and now walks with the aid of twin sticks, albeit customised as befitting the lynchpin of a rock-music gathering.

Dom still remembers the way his childhood bedroom was basically his whole world. He painted giant murals on the walls as a teenager and is still addicted to playing video games. 'I started crawling at the age of 12,' he recalls. 'Then, when I was 14, my grandma bought me a drum kit and it changed everything.' Soon after he went to his first gig – a metal band called Breed 77 at the Adelphi Club in Hull.

Dom always knew he wanted to do something creative and harboured an early ambition to be an actor. He studied theatre at college – often wearing skirts and full make-up. No wonder, then, that he landed a gig in a Marilyn Manson tribute band. Following a series of internships with magazine publishers in London, he enrolled in a master's in magazine journalism. On the first night out of the new academic term, he met a girl at a local nightclub.

'It all comes down to my dance skills,' he laughs. 'I'm a killer on the dance floor. No, really, man. I've got some moves.'

The girl had dreadlocks and piercings – and an 8-year-old son. 'You find all the girls with issues in the Goth scene,' grins Dom.

They started a relationship that continued, despite long distances and assorted pressures, for several years. 'I'd always thought, "No way, not the kids thing,"' he recalls. 'But it became increasingly important to move in together and strengthen the family unit. I wanted to take responsibility for them.'

He still recalls the first evening he spent with Stacey and Xander. 'I was reading him a bedtime story about pirates and I was doing all the voices. He was draped across me and it felt oddly comfortable. To this day,' he says, suddenly serious, 'it's still one of the defining moments of my life.'

Serious bit over, he laughs again: 'I guess 2008 Dom is just very different to 2016 Dom.'

And tales of rock 'n' roll excess are behind him now. 'My life has done a complete U-turn. For me, it becomes less of a challenge every day.'

'But my parents still don't understand why I chose this path,' he says. 'My mates are still going out and playing gigs. Nobody else gets it.'

'But it's okay,' he adds. 'I know they're just looking out for me.'

Teenage rebellion

Today Dom runs a series of businesses, including an online music magazine, *Soundsphere* (www.soundspheremag.com); a marketing agency for the music industry, Creative Condition (www.thecreative-condition.co.uk); and a consultancy for disabled entrepreneurs, for which he picked up the award for entrepreneurial excellence at the National Diversity Awards 2012. He regularly delivers inspirational talks to the delegates of Naidex, a trade and consumer show dedicated to the lifestyle of people with a disability or impairment.

But Dom's role as a father is both his biggest challenge and greatest achievement so far. The best moment as a stepfather? He ponders for a moment, and then breaks into a smile. 'Taking Stacey and Xander to a music festival in Budapest,' he says. 'That was cool, man.'

There have been tough times, of course. Dom and Stacey have felt their relationship being tested on several occasions, and the challenge of bringing up a young man, previously without a solid father figure, has heaped the pressure on at flashpoints. 'There were moments when I thought, "I'm outta here." Friends have told me about some mythical other life I could be leading. But it was gone in a moment and then I snapped back to reality,' he says.

'I know I couldn't live without Stacey and Xander,' he says. He swirls the tea in his mug then fixes me with his baby blues. 'Growing up is growing up. You've got to live it and make new dreams. You've got to stick with it. It took four to five years to adapt to the idea. It was a massive adaption but, when I turned 30, I felt the moment had come.'

And now? 'I'm here for the long haul – the rest of my life,' he says. 'I'm responsible for them now and would never leave them.'

But, for all the joys of fatherhood, stepping into an authority role with another man's son is no easy task.

'I'm not a stereotypical disciplinarian,' he says. 'But that's what not being a dad by blood does for you – it lets you stand back and take stock more. Stacey has a problem with my parenting skills. She says I need to get better. I'm not advising anyone to follow my model of parenting, but, still, it seems to work for me.'

'I feel like I'm on Xander's wavelength,' he adds. 'We talk about video games, comic books and music. Our dynamic is pretty chilled out. He's just a good kid with a taste for rebellion.'

'Having said that, it's a constant battle to not be the friend,' he adds. 'I'm not always comfortable with the role but being a parent and getting him to listen to me is what I've got to do. Hell, I didn't even know I had this authoritarian voice inside me.'

Dom knows it's a work in progress. With Xander in his early teens, there's still a long way to go. 'You have to invest, to graft, to learn to be a dad. There has to be compromise,' he says. 'I've had to learn the definition of parenting. Although it wasn't a word I was particularly comfortable with.'

As he's talking, I think about my own approach to parenting: the way, before divorce, I always used to be the nice cop and how, afterwards, I had to be the nasty cop, too. It was never a role I felt comfortable with and one, probably due to the stress of the situation, I fear I sometimes overplayed.

Dom knows that feeling, too. But sometimes he feels he is getting through. 'He's a teenager now but, despite the anger, he still tells me sometimes that he loves me and admires me.

'The next minute,' he adds, 'he's talking about how he has about five girlfriends on the go at the same time. They all seem to be called Abby, Abs or something.'

Growing up

Looking to the future, Dom knows there are pitfalls ahead – in particular, the way that his free-form working routine regularly clashes with the more rigid rhythms of family life. 'I know Stacey just wants a normal life,' he says. 'We're a super-strong unit but, while I've changed my character, I can't change the creative way I work.'

'I did try getting a job in Lush once,' he adds. 'I thought I'd smell nice.'

Dom accepts that it's an ongoing story but he's not resentful of the way his life has changed – far from it. 'I took a risk and I continue to do that to make my life worth living. I'm fully invested as a stepdad,' he shrugs. 'I guess I'm just in full-on dad mode.'

I know how he feels. There have been times when I have let things go – work, friends, opportunities – but I simply chose my daughters. Being with them when they were little felt more important to me. Like Dom, it was my choice.

We're finishing our tea and the bearded hipsters are carrying designer-chic trays laden with overpriced focaccia for the start of the lunch rush. The soundtrack around us is shifting from gentle acoustic ballads to a more up-tempo beat. Before we head off, Dom tells me about an early Christmas present from Stacey and Xander – a comic book of their story as a family.

'I take it with me everywhere now,' he grins. 'We're all sat on the sofa together, watching *Deadpool* and playing video games.'

He grins again. 'It has been a six-year learning curve,' he adds. 'But it's cool, man. Love changes everything.'

Dad tips

Being a stepfather is about being the dose of reality. You have to be prepared to put in the graft.

A stepfather role gives you a good perspective and room to stand back, balancing being responsible with a sense of separation. I'm 80% stepdad and 20% friend.

Stepfamily facts

- There were 544,000 stepfamilies with dependent children in England and Wales in 2011.
- The number of stepfamilies – a category which includes both married and unmarried parents – in England and Wales increased by 14% in the decade up to the 2011 Census.
- Over the same period – which saw a soaring birth rate – the total number of families with dependent children rose by 150,000 to 4.3 million.
- Of the 4.2 million children in England and Wales, 35% do not live with both parents.
- Nearly a third of all couples bringing up children have a child from an earlier relationship in their family.
- The growing number of stepfamilies means that nearly two million children in England and Wales live in a two-parent family – but with one parent who is not their own.
- In 2016 there were 18.9 million families in the UK.

Sources: Office for National Statistics (www.ons.gov.uk); www.telegraph. co.uk; Aviva Family Finances survey, reported in the *Daily Mail* (www. dailymail.co.uk)

Reflection

A recurring theme in Dom's story is about growing up, and it reminds me of something the apostle Paul writes: 'When I was a child, I talked like a child, I thought like a child, I reasoned like a child. When I became a man, I put the ways of childhood behind me' (1 Corinthians 13:11).

Fatherhood has a way of jolting us men out of our childish ways and propelling us into maturity, and becoming a stepdad to an 8-year-old son could not be described as a gentle introduction to the art of paternity. You're in the deep end from the word go, and like many fathers Dom entertained thoughts of quitting, moments when he could have reverted to childlike behaviour – giving up, storming off, sulking. But instead he has decided to choose the narrow, rugged path of maturity, and stay put. He is a man who has placed the ways of childhood behind him. He talks differently, thinks differently, reasons differently, and sometimes it startles him. 'Hell, I didn't even know I had this authoritarian voice inside me,' he says.

It's surprising what we can discover inside ourselves, and fatherhood can trigger all sorts of questions that lead to moments of self-discovery. Perhaps it is because we are no longer only thinking about ourselves; we have somebody else, for whom we're responsible, to consider. For the first time, we may begin to ask ourselves what life is all about. Why am I here? What should I be doing? Where am I going? What do I want for my children? And the possibility of God can cross our minds. In the past, God may have seemed a childish notion, the stuff of Sunday-school lessons and superstitions; but now we are fathers he begins to make more sense.

God is our Father and perhaps it is our own fatherhood that makes us understand and value him more – just like properly appreciating our earthly parents when our children come along. As Mark Twain said, 'When I was a boy of 14, my father was so ignorant I could hardly stand to have the old man around. But when I got to be 21, I was astonished at how much he had learned in seven years.'

The maturity fatherhood brings can make us see things differently, and believing in God can begin to seem a less childish concept. The good news is that God's love knows no limits, and there is always a forgiving welcome for those who have previously rejected or neglected him. God loves us through thick and thin.

Fatherhood is all about love, and when Dom says at the end of his story that love changes everything, I don't think he's referring to the kind of love that makes you doe-eyed and causes your heart to beat faster. The words Dom uses to describe his love for his family are 'compromise' and 'graft' and 'responsibility'. He is a mature man working at being a great dad, and he is there for 'the long haul'. It's a philosophy of fatherhood he shares with God.

2

Turnaround dad – Scott

A recovered heroin addict finds that faith and fatherhood offer him a new way forward after years of self-destructive behaviour. But the little voice inside is never far away.

'It's all about identity and purpose,' says Scott, his world-weary face furrowed like a favourite cushion. 'Who am I and what is my purpose?'

'That,' he sighs with the air of a man who has seen more of life than a man in his 40s should have, 'is the root of most of my difficulties, from my schooldays onwards.'

Those 'difficulties' led Cumbrian-born Scott, via 20 years of substance abuse, 15 years of living on the streets and periods in and out of prison for petty theft and shoplifting, to a rehab centre in Colwyn Bay in North Wales.

He was 35 years old and about to relapse, again.

'I'd been clean for two months and I felt great. I was attending Alcoholics Anonymous and Narcotics Anonymous and I was praying,' he remembers. 'Then I bumped into an old contact in KFC in Colwyn Bay and they gave me a bag of stuff.'

'It was the darkest night of my life,' he adds. 'I was back in hell.'

But Scott survived. He went on to meet his wife, Sian, at the local church, part of the Alliance of Welsh Churches. Blonde, blue-eyed Emily was born in 2013. Scott started teaching adult education courses and completed a postgraduate certificate in education, working primarily with the social-justice charity Nacro. He was named Teacher of the Year in 2015, picking up an Inspire Award from the National Institute of Adult Continuing Education (NIACE), a charity that promotes adult learning.

'My identity and purpose have changed dramatically in the last few years,' says Scott. 'I'm a husband, a father and a son now. I'm a new man.'

Scooterist revival

I meet 43-year-old Scott at his home in Llandudno, Wales, and find him tinkering in his shed with his two Lambretta motor scooters. A sign on the door reads: 'Dad's Shed: Genius At Work'.

'It's not a midlife crisis,' he assures me, pulling back the covers to reveal a seriously collectable series two scooter and a GP TS1. 'I feel that, since Emily was born, I've made the scooters an idol in my life, so I've decided to sell one of them; I don't need them to fill the God-shaped hole any more,' says Scott, who is dressed casually in a blue Bench T-shirt and faded jogging bottoms.

'I've spent my whole life searching for a purpose – from drugs to scooters – but it was there all along.'

Emily was born at the Glan Clwyd hospital in a room filled with worship music. Scott describes how a dove sat on the windowsill throughout the delivery as a manifestation of the Holy Spirit, and a wicker dove now sits above the sofa in the dining room. A DVD of the film *Quadrophenia*, the story of a young man's road to redemption, sits knowingly on the shelf nearby.

'Becoming a father brought joy and fear at the same time,' Scott recalls. 'I could hear the niggling voice inside my head saying, "You can't do this," and all the old insecurities started flooding back in.'

'But I looked at Emily and she was so perfect. I knew I wanted her to be strong,' he adds. 'I knew we would pray with her and break this cycle of addiction together to set her on the right path in life.'

Today Scott works closely with recovering addicts and firmly believes that addiction is a heart disease that needs a spiritual cure. 'When we see kids start experimenting with substances, then we should listen and, ultimately, pray for them. I share my own experiences when God calls upon me to do so and I may share them with Emily one day – when a learning moment comes. After all,' he smiles, 'I've done all the things she could possibly ever do.'

'As parents,' he adds, 'our job is to lay the foundations. If, or when, it hits the fan, Emily can call on those truths from the foundations we have laid together as a family.'

Darkest hour

Over bowls of homemade soup and ham sandwiches around the dining table, Scott tells me about his lowest point, when he relapsed into heroin use while in rehab in October 2008. Billy the cat ambles through the room as Scott describes the longest night of his life.

'My room was very bare – I arrived at rehab with just two carry bags,' he recalls, gesturing around the cosy family room we're sitting in, the fireplace topped with a statue of an angel and a set of bongos on the floor. A card on the sideboard says 'Cherish' and a book leaps out from the bookshelf on account of its title, *Everybody's Normal Until You Get To Know Them*.

'I'd got the stuff from an old contact at KFC and then found some foil from somewhere back at the rehab place and smoked it. I went down to dinner that night with my head up my bum but I covered it. I was out of it but you get used to coming up with excuses as an addict,' he says.

'But this time it didn't give me the usual hit. I was itching all over and the waves of sickness were coming over me as soon as I had smoked it. The feelings of guilt were even worse. All the years on the streets were easy, topped up on booze and drugs, but being in an old hotel with 21 rooms and 21 people all at different stages of the recovery programme was really hard,' he adds.

'Looking back,' Scott smiles, 'that was the best bag of heroin I ever had, as it opened my eyes to life. I was in hell afterwards and I couldn't look anyone in the eye. So, after five days, I decided to knock on the manager's door and tell the truth. They made me wait all day in a bare room, cold and shaking, before they called me in for their decision.'

Scott gets quite emotional describing how, instead of just sending him back out on the streets, the manager decided to give him 28 days to sort himself out before leaving the rehab centre. 'Afterwards I went up to my bedroom, got down on my knees and cried out to God, "I can't do this any more!" I went into repentance alone in my room, raising my arms in the air and crying it all out. It wasn't a road-to-Damascus moment but it was my moment. I just lay down afterwards and slept.'

'When you first try heroin, people say it's like being kissed by God himself. I still remember the feeling – even now,' says Scott. 'It was like being wrapped in cotton wool. All addicts spend their lives trying to recapture the feeling of that first hit. But, that night, for the first time since I'd used heroin aged 20, I experienced that feeling of being enveloped in love – God's love. That night I truly was kissed by God himself.'

'Looking out the window the next morning,' he recalls, eyes still dewy from the powerful memory, 'I knew I had stopped.'

Self-help

These days Scott still carries the battle scars of addiction with him daily. He has dints in his head where he was beaten and a hole in his groin from injecting.

But he has channelled his own experiences into a more positive outlet, helping other recovering addicts through his new education and intervention organisation, 4:28 Training (www.428training.com). The courses he delivers, aimed at adults with a history of substance abuse, petty crime and homelessness – the hard to reach – include digital literacy, employability skills and interpersonal development.

Scott still remembers, however, the feelings of dislocation, a sense of trying to fit in that he traces back to the age of 12, when his parents moved him around schools in Warrington and he took to smoking, drinking and doing drugs behind the bike sheds as a way to be accepted by his peers.

'I remember when I was sleeping rough in a doorway on Charring Cross Road in London and watching all the "normal" people going by with their cars, homes and holidays. I felt I would never be accepted as normal,' he says, the weariness evident around his hazel eyes and his cropped, dark hair half covering a deeply furrowed brow.

'There's a voice inside still challenging my identity,' he adds. 'The more I step into my new identity as a father, the more those flaming arrows still attack me.'

'I existed for 18 years between periods of absolute despair and the utterly mundane,' he says. 'It took just one week for me to get addicted to heroin but 18 years to get off it. I realise now that addiction is very selfish: it's all about making me feel better about me.'

'What's different now is that I have a very dear relationship with Jesus and I have a family. It feels amazing. The enemy still breaks in now and then; I still have fears and uncertainties on certain days but, whenever the enemy challenges my identity and purpose, I know God tells me that I am loved,' says Scott.

'My identity now is in Christ. My purpose is to be in a relationship with him. My feelings towards him are pure love. That's why, when I look at Emily now, I understand what unconditional love is. Through her, I now know that God loves us unconditionally.'

'I've discovered my true identity and purpose. What's more,' he says, 'I've learned not to define myself by my past.'

Dad tips

Make the most of the time you have with your children. Once it's gone, it's gone.

Don't let the hurts of your childhood affect your relationship with your kids. Do all that you can to make peace with your past.

Build up a network of supportive friends – other dads that can be there for you (and you for them).

Addiction facts

- 86%: young people in specialist services who say they have a problem with cannabis
- 51%: young people in treatment seeking help for alcohol misuse in 2015, declining from 67% in 2010
- 89%: young people accessing specialist substance misuse services with concerns around the use of new psychoactive substances, also known as 'legal highs'
- 1,340: those in contact with services for the problematic use of ecstasy
- 26%: proportion of young people referred to specialist substance misuse services from education providers, nearly reaching that from youth-justice services (29%)
- 25%: girls aged under 15 in treatment, compared to 19% of boys
- 12%: girls reporting sexual exploitation when presenting to treatment services
- 80%: proportion of the 12,074 young people leaving services who did so in a planned way, no longer requiring specialist treatment

Source: Public Health England's National Drug Treatment Monitoring System (NDTMS) (published December 2015)

Reflection

The prophet Jeremiah asked whether a leopard can change its spots; it can't do it by itself, but with God's help anything is possible. Scott's story proves it. All of his words are so compelling it is hard to pick any out, but there is a short sentence that leaps off the page and confronts me with an unquantifiable amount of hope.

'I'm a new man,' Scott says.

Scott has changed, and change is perhaps the most powerful force in human existence. Intentional positive change can renew, revitalise, refresh and transform a person, and affects not just that person but everyone around them. The Holy Spirit – God who works deep within our hearts and souls – is a provocateur of change, and when we surrender to the Holy Spirit's influence I am in no doubt that we will change. It's inevitable. It could be instant but more likely it will be a slower burn, so we may not always notice how we are changing.

Although there is a dramatic and powerful moment in Scott's story when, alone in his room in the hostel, he gets down on his knees and cries out to God, it seems that not all the change was done there and then. Perhaps it was just the start. Maybe that was the point at which Scott sincerely opened his heart to God and accepted that God loved him. And it gave the Holy Spirit the foothold that was needed to begin the process of change within him.

It says in 2 Corinthians 5:17 (The Living Bible): 'When someone becomes a Christian, he becomes a brand new person inside. He is not the same anymore. A new life has begun!' Scott clearly articulates that he is a follower of Christ, a Christian. He says, 'My identity now is in Christ. My purpose is to be in a relationship with him.' So Scott has become a new person. He is not the same any more. 'I've learned not to define myself by my past,' he says. And in that statement, he doesn't deny the years of drug-taking and crime; he doesn't pretend it hasn't happened, but he refuses to let it control his future. He is a new Scott, and part of that newness, as well as following Christ, is being a father to Emily.

I sense that Scott is still changing, even now. His decision to sell his beloved scooter is evidence of that, and it seems his role as a father has caused him to question his devotion to his Lambrettas. I wonder if fatherhood always brings with it choices to change or stay the same? We can be the men we were or we can allow fatherhood to change us and keep changing us. Scott has spent much of his life indulging, by his own admission, selfish desires, but now he has changed and is still changing, and he is nobly choosing to make sacrifices for the sake of his daughter. Scott is loving Emily in the same way his Father in heaven showed love for him when he cried out ,'I can't do this any more!'

Jesus said, 'With man this is impossible, but with God all things are possible' (Matthew 19:26). There is no denying that God has changed at least one leopard's spots.

3

Midlife dad – Darren

Coming to a major crossroads in life proved liberating for a man driven by a desire to give something back. But how would his family react to him turning his back on the breadwinner role?

Darren always loved a good game: Monopoly, Top Trumps, Operation.

But it was Yahtzee that he loved most of all.

'I have very vivid memories of playing Yahtzee with my granddad in a council house in North Wales aged 5. It feels very comforting, even now,' he says, eyes gleaming from behind thin-rimmed glasses as the warm glow of childhood fills the room.

'I also remember a rainy holiday in the Lakes aged 7 and spending the whole time playing Battleship with my brother,' he adds. 'It was a time when we had no worries or pressure.'

Darren is in his mid-40s now – but he still loves a game of Yahtzee. These days, however, he plays with his two teenage sons, Ethan and James.

'Men in particular like to play and have fun. We should embrace that,' says Darren. 'I think there's a place for more play in life, especially between grandfathers, dads and sons. An added dimension for me is now sharing the comfort and joy I felt as a boy with my own sons.'

Play date

I meet Darren in the kitchen of his family home. He took redundancy from a well-paid job in IT some six months ago and, despite halving the family income, he looks relaxed in a striped T-shirt and shorts. The house is filled with the sights and sounds of family life on a sunny morning: scooters parked by the front door, a music stand set up in the front room and a selection of recipe books open on a kitchen shelf.

'The redundancy payout started some momentum to cut ties. It felt like things were starting to fall into place, working towards something new while also securing the family,' he says. 'I always had an idea to start something to help communities in need and it was time to explore that more.'

The new venture is a community-interest company, WACE (Your Way Your Place – wace-chester.org.uk), based out of an old church building in North Wales. It will ultimately comprise a cafe and activity space, using money generated to fund community projects. The budget is around £350,000 to see the idea through to completion.

'I came up with the idea of a place for families to come together, play games and take challenges. We always played games together at work and home, daft things like

Professor of play

The University of Cambridge recently appointed the world's first professor of play.

The appointment, Paul Ramchandani, a researcher in child and adolescent mental health, was funded through a £4 million grant from the Lego Foundation, the charitable arm of the toy company.

Professor Ramchandani will explore how play can support education, promote emotional well-being and equip children with positive skills through play-based teaching.

He said, 'There has been a lot of research on play generally. But understanding how it fits in with other areas of child development, as well as how to use it in children's education, has been under-researched.'

Source: www.theguardian.com/higher-education-network

spin the orange and building towers of playing cards,' says Darren. 'I believe that when we interact, we build something – like corporate team-building but more fun.'

Working life

For Darren, the opportunity to start over felt liberating, especially after 15 years of the daily grind. 'I wouldn't have said this at the time but, looking back, my working life felt like survival on a battlefield. I was just trying to get through the day,' says Darren. 'I think the pressure of the modern workplace is far greater than before. The culture of never being appreciated and the bosses playing the blame game left me constantly on the defensive.'

'I brought that home with me each night. It did, of course, at times cause friction with my family,' he adds. 'My ability to disconnect from work in the past was not great.'

But since leaving work, he has found a new lightness to life. He can breathe again.

'Of course there's a fear of jumping into the abyss. But, for me, making these decisions feels like taking more control over my life as a man. I have the freedom in my head to enjoy life more,' he says.

'I feel like the old me. I thought we would worry more about money and what tomorrow may bring but, in fact, I feel more able to take life day by day. Now I try to listen and not react, not take things so personally. If you are calmer, then people will react to you more calmly,' he adds.

The shift in work–life balance is, according to Darren, having a positive impact on family life, too, and his role is shifting from simply provider to actually being a father to the boys and a husband to his partner, Sarah.

'Parenting felt quite burdensome at times. Now I'm really enjoying it,' he says. 'We send the boys off to school with less stress. I have the space and time to talk to them about their day.'

'Making changes', he adds, 'can impact very positively on your mental health and relationships.'

Crisis management

Being in midlife myself, I, like many men in this age group, have moments of self-doubt and times when a sense of futility takes hold. Talking to Darren across the kitchen table is making me think about how a long commute to work several days a week affects the way I react to the people I love. I get the treadmill scenario only too well.

But some people could take a more cynical view. A man in his 40s asking where did it all go wrong. Surely it's just a short hop on to buying a pair of leather trousers and straddling a Harley Davidson, or recreating scenes from the film *American Beauty* by rediscovering your teenage vinyl collection and pumping iron in the garage in between tokes on herbal cigarettes.

After all, the optimum age for a man to experience some kind of midlife crisis is from 40 to 59, according to 2016 research by the Office for National Statistics. 'The stakes are higher at this stage in your life than any other,' says therapist Andrew G. Marshall, author of *It's Not a Midlife Crisis, It's an Opportunity: How to be 40 or 50-something without going off the rails*.

Darren refutes the idea of another male midlife crisis. 'I see friends who are now a mirror image of what I was like a few years ago. I don't think I've got something they haven't. I just have the time and space to listen and ask questions better,' he says.

'Some men,' he adds, 'treat this period in their lives as an opportunity to re-evaluate themselves with complete disregard for the people around them. But I think you can make it a very positive experience. You can harness it to make changes.'

'Maybe it will become a hard slog. Maybe the first six months will bring financial pressure to bear. But I hope it will help me be a better person,' he smiles. 'This project has a community, not a financial, feel.'

Another motivation throughout this period of transition has been Darren's faith. He says, 'It did feel like standing at a crossroads, a time of affirmation. The way things came together in a particular order at a particular time were signposts, leading me down a certain path. I took things along the way as signs.'

'All the conversations I was having felt like they had a purpose. New ideas, previously hidden under the surface, were fizzing to the top like a glass of champagne,' he adds. 'It felt like a higher force propelling me forward.'

Yet, while the project is born out of faith, WACE is not a Christian project per se. 'Faith is part of every day. If I didn't believe we had been chosen to run this project, then I would have given up on it long ago. We are starting something that will grow far bigger than us,' he says.

'My prayers are thoughts, not in the sense of words,' he adds. 'We have faith and feel chosen to do it, but we're not going to tell people they are doing something wrong.'

Future plans

Back at the kitchen table, we're on our second mugs of tea, placed on a tablecloth with the slogan 'Dad's world famous hotdogs'. The contents of the laundry basket are still waiting for a blow out on the line in the summer breeze.

It's still relatively early days for the project but already the dreams are big. Darren hopes it will be a blueprint for other spaces in deprived areas around the UK, all based around community projects and themes of food, creativity and art. He aims, ultimately, to draw a modest salary from it and create jobs for people in the community.

'We want to create the spaces, then bring in people from the community to run them in their own way. These centres would be well placed to tackle our social issues, such as mental health, isolation, loneliness and communication,' says Darren. 'Third-sector companies now recognise the need to drive their own projects. It doesn't work by someone standing up and telling people what to do.'

'I see more responsibility on people who have the opportunities in life to give back, not just take what they can. I see the rise of local businesses offering proper human interaction and service which focuses on the person,' he adds. 'If we open ourselves up and make ourselves part of the network, then we open up the world to people in the community to allow them to see their ideas come to fruition.'

Most of all, however, the idea of knocking down the Jenga bricks with one sweeping hand gesture demonstrates how, sometimes, we have to be bold to grasp life and shape it. Every man I know has moments of midlife crisis, woven like badges of honour into the fabric of their daily lives. But not many have the drive to tackle the feelings head on and become their master.

'I see the value of structure as a family, but we, as people, we should be able to switch if we're not happy. I'm trying to show my boys how life should be lived. It's about creating foundations from which to make their own decisions in the future,' says Darren.

'I'm demonstrating to the kids that it's okay to aim for something not set in stone, to consider who they are and what they want to achieve in life. I now think of responsibility as something to relish,' he adds.

We drain our mugs of tea. 'The idea of making this project happen makes me feel happy,' says Darren. 'Happy at a very deep level.'

Crisis. What crisis? Besides, it's time for a game of Yahtzee.

Dad tips

Play together. Make time to play something with your little one, even if it's only a short game. It's stress relief for you, and builds skills in your child beyond what you can see.

Share your problems. Too many parents try to 'be strong' in front of their children. Share with them your problems (within reason), discuss solutions and share how you worked through solving the problem.

Be an example rather than point to one. Actions really do speak louder than words.

Ten signs you're having a midlife crisis

- Discontentment or boredom with life (including people and things) that provided fulfilment beforehand
- Feeling restless and wanting to do something completely different
- Anxiety about the future
- Confusion about who you are or where your life is going
- Irritability or unexpected anger
- Persistent sadness
- Increased use of alcohol, drugs or food, or other compulsions
- Sexual affairs, especially with someone younger
- Fretting about status and the point reached in your career
- Questioning decisions made years earlier and the meaning of life

Source: Andrew G. Marshall, *It's Not a Midlife Crisis, It's an Opportunity: How to be 40 or 50-something without going off the rails* (Marshall Method, 2016), andrewgmarshall.com

Male midlife facts

- 43: optimum age for a midlife crisis to hit
- three to ten years: length of a male midlife crisis (compared with five years in women)
- 2% per year (from around the age of 30 to 40): fall in testosterone levels per year as men age. Although this is unlikely to cause any problems per se, it has been linked with the male menopause (sometimes called the andropause).
- 150 minutes: total amount of physical activity required over a week to promote health benefits. Regular physical activity can effect up to a 35% lower risk of coronary heart disease and stroke and up to a 30% lower risk of depression.
- 1965: year the term 'midlife crisis' was first coined to describe the depressing moment when people become aware of their own mortality and realise there is probably less time left to live than the time they have lived so far

Sources: NHS Choices (www.nhs.uk); Office for National Statistics (www.ons.gov.uk); www.mirror.co.uk; www.telegraph.co.uk

Reflection

Have you ever reached a point at which you have realised that your existence has become a seemingly endless routine of commuting, working, driving, cooking and sleeping, and the hope that your life will be momentous and your work will make some lasting difference has deserted you? Yes, you're providing for your family, but you had always wanted to do more; you wanted to leave a more profound legacy. You don't feel valued, and work has become about survival. Is it just a midlife crisis, a phase that just needs to be trudged through, like a more mature version of teenage angst? Or is it God's way of telling us to pause, take stock and ask ourselves serious questions about which route to take from here? As Darren explains, it was for him 'like standing at a crossroads' looking for signs.

At such junctures, many of us ignore the roads to our left and right and just keep straight on, stuffing our feelings further down inside us. Certainty and financial security win the day. Perhaps we deaden the anguish with alcohol or drugs. Others look for fulfilment in a change of appearance, vehicle or partner. Darren's story gives me hope that these, often ultimately unsatisfactory, outcomes are not inevitable. Insightfully, Darren observes that at such moments it is possible for men 'to re-evaluate themselves with complete disregard for the people around them'. But he has chosen to make it a positive experience, to improve his relationships, to make himself a better father and husband.

Shining through Darren's story is the importance of relationships and the part that play has in bringing people closer to one another and improving life. Is it a childish idea? I really don't think so. Perhaps we all have a natural inclination to play, and, if so, why should it be inevitable that it gets weaker as we age? Maybe we simply push it down further inside ourselves and cover it up with the notion that play is a trivial indulgence and that it is much more worthwhile to prioritise work. In the golf film *The Legend of Bagger Vance*, the narrator, Old Hardy Greaves, says, 'God is happiest when his children are at play.' Can it be true? As a father, I can identify with the sentiment as I have always loved to watch my children play, to see them totally absorbed in the business of having fun. I have never taken time out to watch them do their homework but I have regularly watched them play sport or perform playing a musical instrument. Dads love to watch their children play. Knowing my children are happy, seeing them enjoy themselves and hearing them laugh gives me a huge amount of pleasure. So why not God?

Jesus said, 'I have come that they may have life, and have it to the full' (John 10:10). I have a sense that Darren is now living life to the full, helping others live life to the full and passing on to his sons, Ethan and James, what his grandfather passed on to him: a love of play that fulfils him, makes him a better dad and husband, and pleases his Father in heaven.

4

Reunited dad – Chris

A neo-Nazi found that, by renouncing a life built around violence, he could finally find some inner peace and reconnect with his estranged son. But it took a brush with death to start him down a new path in life.

'There was an Asian lad outside the pub. He was drunk and urinating against a wall. So I karate kicked him, put him on the floor and then started laying in.'

Chris sits before me. He is describing how he spent 20-odd years locked into a vicious circle of extreme violence and self-destruction. 'When you have someone around the throat, choking him or her until their eyes are starting to glaze over, well, it's like a drug,' he deadpans. He has a shaved head and a white goatee and sports a black bomber jacket. It's not the typical attire for lunch in the cafe of an East Midlands spiritual retreat.

'I remember the feeling of taking him to within seconds of his own death. The ability to spare him made me feel godlike. I'm not a monster,' he adds, 'but I have done monstrous things.'

For 50-year-old Chris, life has been one long apprenticeship at the school of hard knocks. But it has been transformational. He has recently been reunited with his now 18-year-old son, Callum, and found a new role with Operation Prevent, the Home Office's anti-extremism campaign. He still has no contact with his two daughters.

He leans forward. 'I hated the white traitors, the left-wing do-gooders. I wanted to strike back at the highest echelons of society.' This is,

I sense, a man who knows how to handle himself if an argument about the bill for the lemon drizzle cake turns ugly.

'I've been bottled over the head, driven at, attacked with baseball bats,' he tells me nonchalantly as if reeling off his shopping list. 'I suffered a heart attack, have been hospitalised numerous times and sectioned multiple times over.' His voice softens, a trace of his childhood stammer still lurking in the background.

'I've still got my warrior spirit – but I use different weapons now,' he grins, revealing a row of broken teeth.

In short, Chris is transforming. Look at him now.

'Anger was a mask to the fear – and I was scared of everything,' he says. 'The far right works on fear. But I know now that you can't conquer hate with hate.'

Growing up

Chris takes me back to his childhood, growing up in a tough, white working-class town in south Leicestershire in the early 1970s. Family life was very regimented with his father moving from the army to the police.

'The local kids bullied me each day. My childhood taught me fear and hate,' he says. 'The 5-year-old me had invisible friends, as they were the only ones who couldn't hurt me.'

Young Chris went on to develop a speech impediment and still remembers the head teacher telling his parents at parents' evening, 'I don't think Chris has the ability to pass a single exam.'

'I asked my policeman dad for help with the bullies but he said his help would only make the bullying worse. I had to take it like a man.

Soon after, I also got my first label from the world, being classed by school as "a bit thick",' he adds.

It was the death of his father that eventually propelled Chris into the abyss.

'I came home from school one day in 1982 to find a huge crashing noise coming from an upstairs bedroom,' he remembers. 'It was my dad having a heart attack and bouncing off the wardrobes. I realised that, when I walked into the room, I'd never smelt death before,' he adds.

'I was overcome with rage against the unfairness as he breathed his last gasp. I simply locked myself in my room, and I remember consciously declaring war on the world,' says Chris. 'I wanted revenge on my bullies – and I had it within months. I wanted to give the world a good hiding. After that,' he adds, 'violence follows wherever you go.'

From the late 1980s it was a downward spiral. First there was the drink, then a £20,000-a-year cocaine habit. Chris became an active member of a football hooligan gang, following England around international matches. He also dabbled in the occult and embraced nationalism, becoming a member of an ultra-violent neo-Nazi group.

'I was searching and really screwed up,' says Chris. 'I knew it was wrong but I couldn't help myself.'

Close encounter

I know that Chris has done bad things in life but I don't feel nervous as I sit opposite him. Strange that. With all the advantages I've had in life, I'm exactly the sort of bleeding-heart liberal that would have been on the receiving end of his size 9 Doc Martens boot back in the day. Yet Chris sits calmly and answers my questions with patience.

He is still. I'm the one sat here today with a restless mind, having brought my own distractions to the meeting. What brought him to this place?

'It was a spring day and I was choosing which of two trees to hang myself from,' he tells me. 'Suddenly, the wind blew me off my feet. When I got up I was euphoric. It was like always watching TV in black and white then, suddenly, changing to HD. I believe this was God getting my attention. It was the spiritual experience that saved me.'

'I went home that morning, got changed and turned up outside an old Baptist church in the pelting rain. I just fell to my knees and cried out for forgiveness,' he adds. 'At that moment I knew that God accepted me for the rotten stinking racist that I was.'

Finding his faith in 2013 helped Chris to turn his life around, and he has now renounced all his far-right connections, touring schools around the Midlands to talk to students about hate crime and radicalisation.

'The fire in my belly has never gone out since,' says Chris. 'I believe I have been called to shout from the rooftops, to share my faith with other men. Before I peddled hate; now I educate in love.'

Family reunion

Callum was born in 1999, and Chris left the family home when his son was just 3 years old. He was, after that, always an absent father until his son reached the age of 14 when, propelled by faith, they started to move towards a reunion. 'I was too busy having my own pity party to take responsibility for my kids,' he says. 'The day I left, I heard him at the letterbox screaming, "Daddy, don't go!"'

'The world tells me I should feel remorse for that separation and should pay back my debt. My answer is that I've not forgotten but

I can't change it. I live in the present moment. I wake up every morning to pick up my cross,' he adds.

When Callum was 16, Chris sat him down and told him about how he had hurt people in the past. Time and faith have healed the relationship. 'These days, my lad and I have some banter and it's all about building things up, not pulling them down. I'm seeing him this weekend and we're going on holiday together for the first time this summer,' smiles Chris.

'I'm not doing this to score points or make amends,' he adds. 'I want to do it and I feel blessed to have the opportunity.'

Heading home

We finish our coffees, and in the car back to the train station I can't help but admire Chris' band T-shirt, which is black with The Sisters of Mercy logo on it. We share memories of listening to the band while growing up – worlds apart. Maybe one day we will go for a pint and put 'Temple of Love' on the jukebox. I'd like to think so. Today, however, he drops me for my train.

'I know all the ways not to be a good dad. But I'm also fortunate to have what I have today,' says Chris. He knows life is no fairy story and has no fairy-tale ending.

'But, for once,' he smiles, 'love really has conquered all.'

Dad tips

Be the superhero. Our children offer unconditional love so being a superhero to our children simply means showing them love, compassion and attention.

Never promise what you can't keep. When we break promises, we make lost generations.

Callum says...

'I grew up with a figure who, if I walked past them in the street, I wouldn't recognise. I felt the times we did spend together were not based on love but rather harassment from my mother. Something was missing. All I wanted was a father figure who truly understood me and who would be there for me – like I had seen in films.

'Growing into my teens, I did start to see my father more often, yet it still felt like I was kept at arm's length. Maybe I was expecting the fantasy of a relationship like the one between other fathers and sons – playing football, spending the day together, or simply spending time talking with each other.

'A dad means something more to me than just my biological father. It is someone who helps guide me on the path of life, helps with my troubles and also enjoys spending time with me out of love.

'Before, I was trapped in the mentality that I was not good enough to earn love from my father. But I have come to realise that, if he can be forgiven by God for the wrongs in his life, I must do the same.

'One of my favourite authors, C.S. Lewis, says, 'There are better things ahead than we leave behind.' This is true for the relationship I now have with my dad.

'Now our relationship is a clean slate. In the last year I have enjoyed and spent more time with my dad than anyone else. All of this wouldn't be possible without the impact of God in both our lives.'

Prevent: the UK's counterterrorism strategy

Prevent addresses three distinct themes:

1 Challenging the ideology that supports terrorism and those who promote it

All terrorist groups have an ideology. Promoting that ideology, frequently on the Internet, facilitates radicalisation and recruitment. A fundamental part of Prevent lies in challenging terrorist ideology and disrupting the ability of terrorists to promote it.

2 Protecting vulnerable people

Radicalisation is usually a process not an event. During that process, it is possible to intervene to prevent vulnerable people being drawn into terrorist-related activity. There are some analogies between this work and other forms of crime prevention.

3 Supporting sectors and institutions where there are risks of radicalisation

A wide range of sectors is helping to prevent people becoming terrorists or supporting terrorism. The way the government works with particular sectors will vary. Priority areas include education, faith, health, criminal justice and charities. The Internet is also included as a theme running through the strategy.

Source: Economic and Social Research Council (www.esrc.ac.uk), 2011

UK hate crime facts

- 1,178: reports of hate crime to Stop Hate UK in 2015–16 – an overall increase of four per cent on the previous year
- 53%: proportion of hate crimes reported in 2015–16 motivated around disability and race, which is broadly consistent with previous years (2014–15, 51%; 2013–14, 54%)
- 2%: increase in incidents involving faith, religion and belief with the most likely reporters being those of Muslim faith
- 50%: increase in cash seizures and stops at ports and airports since the start of Prevent
- 60%: increase in referrals to official de-radicalisation schemes since the start of Prevent
- 100%: increase in the number of hate crimes recorded by regional police forces in the months following the Brexit vote
- 27%: increase in the number of hate crimes across England and Wales alone, with ten force areas reporting rises of 50% or more

Note: Police forces in England and Wales can class five types of racially or religiously aggravated offences as hate crimes: assault with injury; assault without injury; harassment; public fear, alarm or distress; and other criminal damage.

Sources: Stop Hate UK (stophateuk.org); Metropolitan Police (www.met.police.uk); www.independent.co.uk.

Reflection

At one point in the film *Invictus*, Nelson Mandela, played by Morgan Freeman, says, 'Forgiveness liberates the soul. It removes fear. That is why it is such a powerful weapon.' Chris' experiences have been so extreme that it is easy to focus on the shocking incidents of violence, drug-taking, his father's death and his near suicide. But it is his encounters with forgiveness that are the most powerful elements of his story.

You can almost imagine the scene in cinematic clarity: Chris, having reached the lowest point in his life, ready to commit suicide, turning up at an old Baptist church in the pouring rain, falling to his knees, head bent down, tears flowing, begging for forgiveness. And then feeling God's assurance that he was forgiven and accepted, knowing that he wouldn't any longer be bound by a downward spiral of doing things that were wrong.

Chris' bitterness about being bullied and his anger at the unfairness of his father's death covered up fear. 'I was scared of everything,' he says. But then forgiveness blunted Chris' hatred, resentment and fury; it diluted his rage and chased away his fear. Forgiveness liberated his soul. Nelson Mandela was right: forgiveness is a weapon with enormous potency. It can soften the hardest of hearts.

Chris is not only forgiven by his Father in heaven, he has also been forgiven by a boy who screamed 'Daddy, don't go!' Chris' son, Callum, has given his dad a second chance. He has wiped the slate clean and now two father–son relationships have been redeemed: between Chris and his Father, God, and between Callum and his father, Chris.

Saying sorry and asking for forgiveness are not easy. We may never have physically hurt another person or walked away from our family, but no one is perfect; we all make mistakes. We may say the wrong thing, neglect relationships, mislead others or let people down.

Saying sorry may seem like weakness, especially if an apology is due to our children, but it is the opposite. Seeking forgiveness is the key to unlocking the door to a new tomorrow. Saying sorry and being granted mercy engenders respect and restores relationships. It cures and it fortifies.

In his letter to the Ephesians, the apostle Paul writes: 'Get rid of all bitterness, rage and anger, brawling and slander, along with every form of malice. Be kind and compassionate to one another, forgiving each other, just as in Christ God forgave you' (Ephesians 4:31–32).

Chris' life of bitterness, rage, anger, brawling, slander and malice has been replaced with one of kindness and compassion. These are Chris' new 'weapons', and the thread of forgiveness running throughout his story has been the quartermaster. Forgiveness is God's strategy for saving the world. As fathers, if we give forgiveness and receive it, it can save our family relationships too.

5

Absent dad – Steve

A life on the ocean waves brought a young man freedom like the wind. But how can the young father in military service square long periods of absence with his family left behind at home?

There were some 600 family members of navy crew gathered on the jetty. Steve had been away for six months and was scanning the crowd for eye contact with his wife as the ship sailed back into Plymouth after a long deployment in the Royal Navy. His son, Ben, was just seven months old at the time.

'It's the eye contact. And then the embrace,' says Steve, welling up at the memory. This image of the returning sailor has been played out over generations in films and TV series across the world.

'It's all about that moment,' he adds. 'It's the indescribable feeling of "I'm home at last".'

I meet Brighton-born Steve at the offices of Christian Vision for Men (cvm.org.uk) in Chesterfield, an unremarkable split-level building in an out-of-town business park. His mobile, nestled in a leather case, buzzes on the table before us. Steve drinks his tea from a mug with the Marmite logo. On the wall by the stairs, the words 'Your Hallowed Name, may I bear with honour' are written in huge letters.

As Steve relaxes on a sofa in a fleece top and trainers, his curly hair and greying beard remind me of an Action Man naval officer toy I had as a child. He even talks with the easy confidence of a man who has held a senior rank and commanded a group of men.

Steve joined the Royal Navy at 17 and first went to sea as an engineer in 1981. He joined *HMS Southampton* just after the Falklands war and started maintaining weapons systems for the Navy. It was an exciting and rewarding time for a young man who had run away to sea after a brush with punk rock in 1970s Brighton.

'There was lots of cold war stuff, such as following submarines around Iceland, plus a six-month tour of Bosnia, and plenty of disaster relief work in the West Indies,' he smiles, eyes shining.

'We were the first British unit to Sri Lanka after the Boxing Day tsunami of 2004,' he adds. 'I loved every minute of the job. There's danger on an everyday basis from the weather but the camaraderie is amazing. You simply can't find that in any other job.'

Family life

But Steve started to question the lifestyle. With his wife, Helen, at home with two boys under 5, three six-month deployments on *HMS Cumberland* between 1993 and 1995 tested his relationship with his family to a new level.

'You have to shut yourself off from it, especially on the first few days of a new deployment,' he says. 'You put the kids out of your mind during the working day. That's why I never had any pictures of them in my office and why, on a day-to-day basis, I never spoke about my family with work colleagues.'

To ease the pain of separation, the family developed a strict routine for the day dad left home before a Monday sailing: church, tea and then departure on a Sunday evening.

'As soon as the taxi arrives, you want to go,' remembers Steve. 'Then you drive to the ship in complete silence.

'You're getting ready to go to sea on the first day but, on the evening of the first night away, it felt tough,' he adds. 'We had cabins of four-to-six men and little privacy. I remember one guy in particular would have a few beers and get really emotional, wanting to show us all pictures of his daughter.'

'Most of us would take ourselves off to a quiet place and sit alone with our thoughts,' says Steve. 'It sounds soppy but I used to tell the kids to look at the moon and think about how I was looking at the same moon.'

'I sent them postcards from all over the world and wrote them both individual letters. In return, they would send me voice tapes – remember this was pre satellite phones and instant communication,' he adds.

'The tapes got me every time. Those were the moments,' he remembers, 'I'd have to shut the door and put up the Do Not Disturb sign.'

Special time

Steve married Helen in 1987 and within four months of the wedding his ship at the time, *HMS Beaver*, was deployed for six months. He also went back to sea for a six-month deployment three weeks after Ben was born in 1989 and, most challenging of all, took a series of six-month deployments soon after Sam arrived in 1991. Moreover, from 1987, all the ships Steve served on were based in Plymouth while the family lived in Portsmouth.

Steve left the Navy in 2007. Today he works as Operations Director for CVM and is father to Ben, now 27, and Sam, 25. In a naval career spanning some 28 years, Steve calculates that he spent 14 years on ships, with a further two 'weekending' from a shore-based job in Plymouth.

Talking to Steve makes me think back to the days after my daughter Maya was born. I was away a fair bit at that time on magazine assignments, trying to build up financial reserves with a young family suddenly on my hands. That was only a couple of nights per month and I still felt guilty about leaving her. Steve was often working six-month deployments with no means of instant communication.

'I met Helen while she was working as a naval nurse. She understood the lifestyle as she shared that vocation to the Navy,' he says. 'She accepted it fully, although of course it was very hard being separated for long periods.'

'For those of us at sea,' he remembers, 'the guilt was often the most challenging thing. Especially when you know from a letter that they're having a hard time and you're drinking a rum cocktail on a Caribbean island.'

In many ways, however, time at home, rather than away at sea, often proved the biggest source of tension.

'You have to drop back into their routine but often you don't know what their routine is,' remembers Steve. 'The reintegration of a dad back into a parenting role is a very common problem for absent fathers.'

However, Steve says that for them this was never a huge issue as the key to this was honest and frequent communication during the times of separation.

'Then,' he adds, 'you would be back on duty two weeks later. You're just getting over one emotional stress when you go back to another. Why do you think that annual divorce rates for military families are often double civilian rates?'

The family found their own way to manage the situation with Steve citing his wife Helen as the 'emotional anchor' of the family unit.

'When I was home,' he says, 'we were a family and did things together. Some men have to-do lists of DIY or jobs around the house but I tried to invest all my time in being with the boys.'

Dark days

One of the most difficult times came, says Steve, when he found out by letter that Ben was being bullied at school.

'Lying in my pit at night with the curtain drawn were the darkest moments,' he admits. 'There was a sense of guilt for not being there and frustration as a father not being able to help my son.'

'We all need a way to deal with the guilt,' he adds. 'A lot of guys drown it in beer. The modern Navy is more technically advanced and culturally it has changed a lot, but there's still a work-hard, play-hard mentality. Personally, I just used to run a lot around the ship, thinking and praying all the time.'

Ben's bullying was followed by bouts of depression as a teenager. Even Sam, the more gregarious of the two boys, showed signs of struggling with the long absences.

'Ben never said he felt abandoned but I couldn't help feeling guilty that, if I'd been around, it might have been different,' says Steve, suddenly pensive.

'Sam, I later found out,' he adds, 'used to take my postcards to bed and read them over before going to sleep. Neither have ever shown any bitterness or anger towards me being away, but clearly they were both working through it in their own way.'

Positive outlook

Maybe Steve and his family were lucky. They maintained a positive perspective on the lifestyle they had chosen and, to this day, attribute a large part of this to the support of the Naval Christian Community.

'The group,' says Steve, 'were people who had been there, done that and bought the T-shirt. There were times of separation when I would cry out angrily at God. But the community provided strength to catch you when it's all going wrong.'

As part of this, other men would sometimes take an informal paternal role with the children of serving fathers while they were away. Steve remembers how a family friend would sometimes take the boys out with his own children and offer 'a steadying influence'.

Rather than feeling jealousy, he insists he remains 'grateful' for the physical presence of another man. 'It's a constant challenge within the community for us, as dads, to provide that role-model figure to boys who need it,' he says.

But even with a strong support network around them, there were times when Steve lost the plot. On one occasion he was doing anti-submarine work and pulled into a high-security base in Scotland. Security was so tight that no one was allowed off the ship to call home.

'I stood on the upper deck that night and shouted at the sky, "If you want this for me and my family, then you can stick it!" Afterwards,' he recalls, 'I had a sense of God saying, "You done now?"'

Looking back

Now decidely on terra firma and with the boys grown up and starting young families of their own, Steve has the benefit of hindsight to consider the big question: was it worth it?

'Yes,' he says without hesitation. 'On a professional level, I know we made a difference and, being a Christian at sea, it put me in a unique position to offer advice and support to young men and women.'

'What's more,' he adds, 'my family are strong and my two boys have a lovely Christian faith. If they'd gone off the rails, then maybe I'd give you a different answer.'

We're finishing our tea in the office, a rough wooden cross on the wall behind us. On the opposite wall is a poster of the boxer Muhammad Ali with the message 'Champions are made from something, and they have deep inside them a device, a dream, a vision.' Downstairs, by the entrance, a film poster for *Rocky* carries the tagline 'His whole life was a million-to-one shot.'

Steve knows there are lots of dads today – serving in the military, in prison, separated from their families for whatever reason – facing the challenges he has faced. He dealt with it as best he could.

But was he a good dad?

'Yes,' he answers, again without hesitation.

'I believe I was and still am. Within the circumstances,' he adds, 'we simply did the best we possibly could, but without our Christian faith and trust in God it would almost certainly have been a different story.'

Dad tips

Communication: be honest and open about what you're feeling while you're apart.

When you're home and with the family, give them your undivided time.

You've got to fit in with their routines and what they're doing.

Ben says...

Ben Martin, 27, is currently working at St Alkmund's in Derby as the (lay) pioneer minister, working with the 18–30 group.

'Being raised in a military family is something totally unique. For all the difficult times when I missed Dad, there are also irreplaceable memories and friends. It was tough at times but, as a parent myself now, I look back and have the utmost admiration for my mum and dad.'

'I had a tough time at school, but hearing his tapes and reading his letters made me remember he was there. An element of fantasy existed where I'd guess what he was doing, and that escapism helped me get through some difficult times. I can say categorically that I have learned so much from the dedication my dad had, and still has, towards our family and his Saviour. It's helped to shape me into the bloke I am today.'

The emotional cycle of deployment

Stage 1 Anticipation of loss: four to six weeks before deployment

Stage 2 Detachment and withdrawal: final days before departure

Stage 3 Emotional disorganisation: early days after departure

Stage 4 Recovery and stabilisation: second month after departure onwards

Stage 5 Anticipation of homecoming: one to two months before return

Stage 6 Renegotiation of the relationship contract: early days after homecoming

Stage 7 Reintegration and stabilisation: four to six weeks after homecoming (sometimes longer depending on type of deployment)

Source: Naval Families Federation (www.nff.org.uk)

Armed services facts

- 10.2%: female representation in the UK Regular Forces
- 11.5%: total female intake into the combined UK Regular Forces and the Future Reserves 2020
- 7%: Black, Asian and Minority Ethnic (BAME) representation in the UK Regular Forces
- 5.8%: Total BAME intake into the combined UK Regular Forces and Future Reserves 2020

Source: Ministry of Defence, UK Armed Forces Biannual Diversity Statistics (1 October 2016)

Reflection

There is something about Steve's story that makes me think of Jesus. It's not David's description of Steve's curly hair and beard or Steve's leadership of groups of men. I think it's the moment when Steve cries out to God in desperation and with complete honesty, 'If you want this for me and my family, then you can stick it!'

It reminds me of when Jesus, just before dying on the cross, cries out, 'My God, my God, why have you forsaken me?' (Mark 15:34)

Steve feels powerless. He is away from home on a ship and when he reaches a base he thinks he will be able to phone his family, but he is not allowed on to dry land and the chance to speak to his loved ones is snatched from him. Jesus' life is taken from him by the unjust actions of others and he too is desperate. Both challenge God. Neither deny he exists, but both seem to feel God is somehow absent. He has led them or allowed them into situations they don't want to be in and then apparently deserted them.

I wonder whether Steve's son Ben felt something similar when he was being bullied. I expect he felt powerless, but did he have any sense of the absence of his father, even though he says he never felt abandoned? I don't know, but it's clear from Steve's words that he himself felt the strain of separation and thought his boys would have experienced it too. There is no denying that Steve was physically absent for long periods of time, but how about emotionally and spiritually? I think that throughout his story there are clues that he was a father who never left his children.

Steve tells us that he thought about his boys a lot and a way of connecting those thoughts with theirs was to look in the night sky, each knowing that they were gazing at the same moon. Steve sent them postcards from all over the world and wrote individual letters to each of them. He says he prayed for them as he ran around the ship, and when he was home he put the list of DIY tasks to one side and spent as much time with them as possible. It strikes me that these are not indicators of absence but evidence of his presence as a father. He was always with them in mind and soul, even though the physical distance between them was great.

Could the same be true of God? We feel he is a Father who is distant and silent, absent even, but then when we look for clues we begin to identify his presence – markers, through our histories and in our lives, that show he loves us and has never abandoned us. And it is often in this searching that we are drawn closer to him.

Steve's story reminds me that more exists than that which we can touch: Steve's love for his sons and God's love for his children. Both are fathers, both steadfast and both present.

6

Widowed dad – Neil

The tragic death of a young woman left two young boys without a mother and a grief-stricken husband descending into a spiral of depression. Could this newly single father ever recover any sense of normal life for his children – or himself?

'I was,' says Neil, 'living the dream: beautiful wife, gorgeous children, a senior job with a good salary.' He fixes me with his blue eyes from behind designer frames. 'Then,' he says, 'I had lost everything.'

We both shift in our seats. Life continues in the cafe around us with coffee-swilling freelancers tapping at their laptops and Friday-morning shoppers scanning their phones for messages. But for Neil, I feel, life has been on hold for ages – as if treading water amid towering, dark waves and grasping desperately for an elusive life raft.

'It's nearly four years now,' he says, the zip of his sports-chic knitwear glinting in the sunlight streaming in through the windows. 'I had been trying to carry on working and looking after the boys, providing them with some sort of stability, while processing my own grief. But it was unsustainable. I knew that I was very depressed and that it would all come to a head.

'What's more,' he adds, 'I had started to resent God, to resent a world in general that didn't care about us. There's a degree of social isolation that comes with being a widowed father.'

'I felt,' he says, the strain of emotion etched into his face, 'we were quite alone.'

Young family

Dorset-born Neil met his wife, Laura Alejandra (Ale to her friends), on an MBA course at the University of the West of England in 2003. They moved to her home country of Mexico in 2004 and settled in Mexico City for a while. The young couple moved back to the UK in 2007 for Neil's work after he secured a job in a senior management role for an international company involved in heavy industry.

'Ale was working and studying at the time,' he smiles. 'She had a job in international trade with a global American-owned bank. But, back in the UK, she couldn't even get an interview. Meanwhile, I soon found myself working long hours with lots of responsibility and time away in hotels,' he adds.

When Benjamin was born in 2008, soon followed by Joshua in 2010, Ale devoted herself to life as a full-time mother. It was a role, explains Neil, she loved and relished, throwing herself into motherhood while he worked hard to support his young family. The family had found their equilibrium and went about life as normal.

That was, until the cancer. It was April 2011 and their world was about to implode.

'Joshi was six months old and Ale had just finished breastfeeding when the lump appeared,' says Neil, talking openly for the first time about the series of tragic events that led to her death in July 2013 at the age of just 37. 'At first we thought it was just blocked glands, but she was subsequently diagnosed with triple negative breast cancer.'

Ale fought the first round of the cancer and received the all-clear later that year, but the cancer returned in 2013. This time the condition was much more severe, frustrated by problems they encountered with the medical profession, despite going back and forth to the GP for over twelve weeks. In desperation they eventually went to hospital for a diagnosis.

By the time she moved to a specialist cancer care centre for her final few months, her extended family from both Mexico and the UK at her bedside, the cancer had spread to her lungs, brain, breast, liver and bones. 'People often have a romanticised view that a cancer patient can go off and live a dream life in the sun for their final few months. We had thought we could do that, residing on Acapulco beach and living an idyllic, simple life for those final months. But in reality,' says Neil, 'people are bed bound, their bones fragile. They need morphine and 24-hour nursing care. Ale had broken both her hips.'

'Ale had become a born-again Christian. She had a strong faith in God,' remembers Neil. 'She decided in the final days that she didn't want chemotherapy. She wanted to fight it with faith, despite my best efforts to convince her to fight it with both drugs and faith. I had to respect her decision. I remember the first oncologist we saw noted on her medical record that I was one of these husbands who didn't want his wife to go through chemotherapy, so wouldn't permit it. Ale was so angry as it was far from the truth. We felt, at times, we had been fighting both the cancer and the system. Ale said it was God telling her to choose a different way.

'Maybe in hindsight,' he adds, 'she just didn't want to put the boys and I through all that suffering. Triple negative breast cancer tends to be terminal – perhaps she had accepted that.'

Single father

After the funeral Neil found himself alone, living away from his own mother and brother, and caring for the two boys – then aged 5 and 2. He admits he struggled.

'I became mum and dad overnight,' says Neil. 'The boys accepted the story of their mum becoming an angel. They were probably too young to understand what was going on.'

'But I felt totally inadequate,' he adds. 'I wasn't emotionally equipped to take the maternal role. I tried to offer them some stability – living in the same house, eating the same mix of Mexican and English food and continuing with life even though Ale was not there. After all, the boys still needed someone to take them to school each day.'

'At the same time, however, I was dealing with my own tragic loss. I felt broken but I had to battle on and provide for my family, going back to work just six weeks later, attempting to hold down a senior job and deliver results for my employer.'

Going back to work offered no distraction from Neil's grief. If anything, it contributed to his stress and his sense of being utterly alone.

'I felt a huge degree of social isolation as a widowed man. I was devoted to my family and my job, so I didn't have a huge social network of people around me,' he says. 'In the subsequent months, I found the few friends we had drifted away. Professionally, business frowns upon the fact you are unable to be at work at 8.00 am, or be in a meeting in a different city first thing in the morning. The other parents at the school, who could see I was struggling, didn't offer to help. The social exclusion had never occurred to me. I had assumed mums would identify with a woman dying of breast cancer.'

His words strike chords with me, as we speak. Although my situation was different, I remember the mothers at the school gate turning their noses up at a single father and the whispering and withering looks. It was as if attitudes were frozen in the 1950s.

'I felt very trapped. I wanted to put my foot on the brake and fix myself,' adds Neil. 'I was the one still living it when everyone else had forgotten.'

Downward spiral

'A few years after Ale died, I was made redundant. This was the last straw, I suppose, the breaking point,' suggests Neil. 'I had been holding it together until this point, despite a series of personal crises. I'd invested years in the organisation but yet again felt let down by the system. Afterwards, I desperately searched for work. I remember being told I was too senior for the jobs I was applying for, and battled with the decision to be honest or not about being a single parent, a widower attempting to achieve a better work–life balance. I started to spiral into a debilitating depression.'

This perfect storm of events was starting to take a toll on Neil's health. He had a hernia, passed a kidney stone, shoulder surgery and even a bout of chicken pox. He remembers times when the boys would find him lying on the sofa, crying and in agony, in the early hours of the morning. 'I think,' he says, 'the grief was coming out of me physically. I couldn't even go to hospital one night as I had to wait for my mother to drive from Bristol. That's when I realised just how isolated I had become.'

Those dark days of depression also took their toll on Neil's faith, one kindled originally by the faith of his late wife. 'I've struggled with faith over the last couple of years,' he says. 'I haven't been brave enough to become an atheist but I definitely had my periods of doubt.

'I know Ale wanted me to bring God into the life of the boys,' he adds. 'But, while I've always tried to respect her wishes, I've found myself at times asking, "If there is a God, then why is he doing this to me?"'

The events of this period clearly damaged Neil as a person. But the circumstances have also served to strengthen his bond with his children. 'Our relationship has changed as a result,' he says. 'The boys hug and cry with me. They are two very sensitive little boys – kind and loving little boys to be very proud of.'

'People say to me, "You're doing a great job." I don't feel like I am but I know we are an emotionally strong group. We are very open, with none of the macho element to the father–son relationship.'

Moving on

It is only in the last few months, after a couple of years experimenting with a combination of counselling and medication, that Neil finally feels he has started to turn a corner. He has stopped drinking alcohol, started exercising regularly and now tries to adopt a more positive, glass-half-full approach to life through mindfulness.

'Maybe I had reached the bottom of the pit and so the only way was up,' says Neil, a fresh round of double-shot coffees on the table before us and the animation of the lunchtime rush infiltrating the quiet corner of the cafe where our conversation has been unfolding.

He recently took the family on holiday to Mexico and came to the decision to move his sons out there permanently. He says he wants to start a new life and open a bistro. 'I really feel I owe it to Ale for my boys to experience living in her culture. Perhaps they'll feel closer to her.'

As for starting a new relationship, he feels he would have to take it very slowly. In many ways, he says, it would just add another layer of complexity. 'But I don't want to be alone for the rest of my life. I miss the companionship and feeling of being in love.'

'My mother says, "You're only halfway through your life,"' says Neil. 'I'm grieving for the loss of someone I still love and yearning for their support, but I know the boys need a mother figure. The boys are getting more inquisitive about their mother as they get older, so by moving to Ale's country, the boys will eventually get to know their mother better.

'For me now,' says Neil, finishing his coffee, 'it's quite simple: I want a better lifestyle and to be with my children. I have subjugated my own well-being for my children over the last few years. I felt I had to. But I'm now looking to achieve a better balance in life.'

'I absorbed all the change and tried to deflect it away from the boys as much as possible, but I'm not a perfect father. I still shout. I still get impatient.'

He finishes his coffee and prepares to head off for the school run. 'I'm not a superhero,' says Neil. 'I just did my best to protect my boys.'

Dad tips

Don't focus on your own grief and loss.

Try not to become isolated.

Try to establish new networks in new environments with new people.

Male mental-health facts in the UK

- Suicide is now the biggest killer of men under 50, accounting for one in four deaths in men under the age of 35.
- Men are more than three times as likely to kill themselves as women.
- One in eight men has experienced a mental-health problem.
- The annual number of suicides among male patients has been increasing since 2006 in England, while for females the number has fallen.
- The rise in male patients aged 45–54 has been particularly striking – around 90% since 2006.
- The number of men currently in treatment for drug and alcohol abuse is three times that of women.
- Men are nearly three times more likely than women to become alcohol-dependent (8.7% of men are alcohol-dependent compared with 3.3% of women).
- Men make up 95% of the prison population; 72% of male prisoners suffer from two or more mental disorders.
- 87% of rough sleepers are men.
- On average, 191,000 men a year report stress, depression or anxiety caused or made worse by work; the peak age group for these conditions is 45–54.
- According to a YouGov survey, 28% of men had not sought medical help for the last mental-health problem they experienced, compared with 19% of women.
- A third of women who disclosed a mental-health problem to a friend or loved one did so within a month, compared with only a quarter of men, according to the same poll.
- People with severe mental-health problems have their life expectancy reduced by more than ten years.
- People with a mental illness are almost twice as likely to die from coronary heart disease as the general population, are four times more likely to die from respiratory disease and are at a higher risk of being overweight or obese.

Sources: Office for National Statistics (www.ons.gov.uk); Men's Health Forum (www.menshealthforum.org.uk); Mental Health Foundation (www.mentalhealth.org.uk); Movember Foundation (https://uk.movember.com); Mind (www.mind.org.uk); The Campaign Against Living Miserably (www.thecalmzone.net).

Reflection

One of the most desolate feelings is loneliness. It can be heart-achingly painful, sucking all the joy and hope from life and leaving you believing you are battling just to exist – maybe not even caring if you exist at all. Neil talks about social isolation but it is when he expresses it in a much more sparse way that the acuteness of his feelings hits home. 'I felt we were quite alone,' he says.

When I read Neil's story I am reminded of Job, who is beset with tragedy and loses much of what he holds dear. Job laments about God: 'He turned out all the lights – I'm stuck in the dark' (Job 19, MSG).

Neil lost his wife, his friends, his job and his physical health, and he says that he suddenly felt he had nothing. The lights went out and Neil too was stuck in the dark. It is no wonder that grief and loneliness led Neil into the gloom of depression.

If depression were a room in a house it would be the cellar – a forbidding place, murky, cold and silent – and we may find ourselves descending there even when we have not experienced the kind of adversity Neil has. Depression is an insidious beast, slinking and slithering its way into our minds, diluting the desires of our hearts and sapping our appetite for life. We may think that as fathers we should feel differently – we should be strong and resilient, emotional mainstays our children can rely on – and it can be tempting to deny our wretched feelings or pretend to others that everything is fine.

What strikes me about Neil is that his honesty and authenticity have strengthened his bond with his boys. His example of vulnerable fatherhood is preparing them to be emotionally sensitive fathers themselves. I believe that they will respect Neil more for seeing him acknowledge his depression and begin to climb the steps out of it.

It is unsurprising that Neil has questioned God. 'If there is a God, then why is he doing this to me?' he cries. And yet I sense in Neil's words that, despite a crisis of faith, somewhere deep within him is a determination to keep believing in God. 'I haven't been brave enough to become an atheist,' he says. Like Job, he may have challenged God, but he has not rejected him.

When the lights are turned out and life leads us into darkness, it is hard to keep believing in God. We cannot make sense of what is happening to us and we may think that even God has deserted us. We feel quite alone. In the face of mounting evidence that seems to suggest God is absent, it is then that we have to fall back on a determination to believe that God is still there, to cling to that belief and not let go. Sometimes it is, quite literally, all the hope we have – but at those moments it is enough.

7

Adoptive dad – Graham

A reluctant father describes how adoption brought new meaning to his life and – finally – taught him how to embrace change.

Graham is a big man: six feet and seven inches in his sporty ankle socks. But he's still not too big to cry.

'We had our first family meal together the day he arrived. Afterwards we put him down to sleep and he started crying,' explains the 40-year-old father of one, cuddling an afternoon-nap-sleepy Alfie, now aged 2, in his penguin pyjamas, before mum Caroline takes him to the kitchen for a snack.

'That's the moment I broke down on the landing. He was sleeping in our house and we were in charge now. It was,' he says, 'the moment of awakening.'

For Cheltenham-born Graham and his wife, Caroline, the road to adoption had been a long one.

'We couldn't have children of our own. We never got to the bottom of why,' he remembers, his rich baritone echoing off the white minimalism of the sitting room.

'We came to the point we felt God was telling us to adopt a child.'

That was 2013. Some six months later, Alfie, then aged 8 months, came to live with the couple permanently.

'He came for the day with his then foster carer. She left around teatime and walked out of his life for ever,' says Graham.

'That,' he adds, 'was the night I lost it.'

All change

I meet Graham, who works in business development, and Alfie in the living room of their house in a suburb of Exeter. The room speaks warmly of the former lives of relatively new parents and the rapid development of their young child.

A quick tour of the bookshelves takes me swiftly from a collection of Ian Fleming novels to a copy of a children's Bible. A photo of Alfie with a dummy in his mouth sits next to a blue rubber duck. A greetings card proclaims, 'You can never have too much togetherness.'

Graham sits squarely opposite me in a grey sweatshirt. A map of the world dominates the wall behind him, so that the Brazilian Amazon appears to be sprouting out of a patch of his sandy hair.

'I don't like change. I don't like putting myself in new situations,' he explains over a mug of tea. 'I like having my own space. Of course, Alfie is exciting and fun and he loves to be around us. But there has been fear too.'

He sips his tea solemnly. 'I feared in the early days I might not enjoy having a child around the house.'

Fatherhood wasn't a given for Graham. Married for 15 years now, the topic of children first came up around ten years ago when their friends started having children. 'Fatherhood was something I'd always assumed would be there in the future but it didn't fill me with a huge sense of longing or joy,' he says.

'I never felt preprogrammed to be a dad. I could have trundled along quite happily without becoming a father.'

While his wife was sure she wanted to have a child, Graham felt the pressure was more social than emotional. 'I remember feeling like an oddity,' he says. 'It was the social impact, rather than an emotional emptiness for me. When you don't have children, there's a part of your friends' lives you can't speak the language of.

'But, of course', he adds, 'my outlook on life has definitely changed since Alfie came along. Children are a great way to knock off the rough spots, and fatherhood has brought out a lot of nurturing instincts towards other people, especially young guys struggling with their own issues. I think that's God's work.'

Absent father

At this point Alfie bursts back into the room. He has just used the toilet for the first time – apparently because the potty felt too cold. And he wants to share the moment with his dad.

'My boy!' exclaims Graham, hugging him.

But another man has missed out on this moment.

When we talk about this man's absence, the room takes on a darker, more sombre tone, despite the brightly coloured kids' toys littering the floor. The afternoon light is fading now; our mood is more reflective. Graham may be a big guy but, in this moment, I can see the little boy still inside.

'We pray for them,' says Graham of the parents who gave Alfie up. 'We're probably 16 years off the day when he may want to track down his birth parents. We will support it as there's probably a lot of healing to come of it. Most of all we want a happy ending. But, for now, I'm as secure in him being my son as he is being my son. He belongs with us.'

The couple met Alfie's birth parents in a contact centre. They knew it would be raw – and it was. 'It was awkward but, at the end, we all hugged. Of course, there were tears. But there was also a lot of grace in the room,' remembers Graham. 'A lot of grace.'

He looked Alfie's birth father in the eye and shook his hand. 'You can't feel guilty,' he says. 'Adopters never feel the child is not theirs. But I do feel sadness for his birth father.'

Sleepless night

Graham believes he's a better person for Alfie joining the family. But, in the months leading up to the adoption, he felt his nerve being severely tested. 'I'd become so wedded to the freedom of a child-free life that I wasn't just ambivalent to being a dad, I was positively hostile,' he says.

'At the same time,' he adds, 'I knew that saying, "We can't do this," was not an option.'

Graham remembers one sleepless night some four months before the couple were finally approved as adopters. 'I was wracked by cold, naked fear about the coming change,' he says. 'It was a lonely place to be. I talked to Caroline but didn't feel I could talk to my male friends about my fears.'

'It was,' he adds, 'God asking me, "Do you trust me?" Looking back, it was an intellectual assent I had to make.'

His admission reminds me of my own fears when I learned my first child was due. I was away with work and, that night, it felt like the loneliest hotel room in the world.

Alfie comes back into the room with a sudden burning desire to play with the toy zoo animals. 'My daddy,' he beams, holding up a giraffe.

It's now some 18 months since Alfie first came into his life, and Graham is still learning to embrace change. At times it's still a bit of a struggle. It takes a big man to admit that, although the tears these days flow from joy, not fear.

'There are times when Alfie tests the limits. And do I miss weekends lounging on the sofa with a box set?' he asks. 'Hell, yes.'

It's time for Alfie's dinner. Graham stands up to his full six-foot-seven frame and takes him in his arms.

'I'm more tolerant, more sympathetic these days,' he says. 'But, most of all, my happiest moments in life are,' he beams, 'quite simply when I'm carrying my boy.'

Dad tip

Be available for your children. I always remember that when my dad was home, he was home.

Adoption facts

- 5,330: number of children in care adopted during the year ending 31 March 2015 – an increase of 5% on the previous year
- 4% (230): number of children adopted during the year ending 31 March 2015 who were under 1
- 36% (1,930): share of the 5,330 children adopted between 1 April 2014 and 31 March 2015 who were part of a sibling group
- 282: number of children matched with families between 1 April 2014 and 31 March 2015 by the Adoption Register for England and Wales

Source: www.adoptionuk.org

Reflection

When we are young we are inclined to believe that we know how life will pan out. Perhaps it is something like this: leave school, study at university, get a job, marry, have children, retire, become a grandparent. Things may not necessarily come in that order but most of the elements will be present at some point or other. We begin to progress through life and everything is going swimmingly; the pattern is taking shape.

But then, like a bolt out of the blue, something unexpected brings us to an abrupt halt. It is not meant to happen and the route we were taking suddenly seems less certain. We peer ahead and all we see is darkness and fog. We are lost.

Although becoming a father was not a passionately held ambition of Graham, he always possessed a quiet expectation that he would, one day, be a dad. It was the path he was on; it was the way things would be.

Then he and Caroline discovered that they couldn't have children, and so Graham adjusted his step and got kind of used to meandering down a new way. Then came the prospect of adoption, and it is at this point in his story that you get the greatest sense of him faltering. The only way ahead is through completely unfamiliar territory and he is, quite frankly, scared. He freezes. He is lonely.

'Do you trust me?' he believes God was asking him, one sleepless night.

It is a question that can return to us, as fathers, time and again throughout life. When we find out we are going to become a father, when we discover we can't have children, when we are struggling to make ends meet, when we face being apart, when we have to let go, when we are about to adopt a child, do we trust God?

Trusting God does not mean dispelling fear. It is not looking at life through rose-tinted spectacles or sticking your head in the sand. It is being aware of the precarious, unpredictable, obscured future and stepping into it anyway. It is taking the next step, and then the next, and making a decision to keep going along the route God is revealing bit by bit.

It says in Isaiah 42:16: 'I will lead the blind by ways they have not known, along unfamiliar paths I will guide them; I will turn the darkness into light before them and make the rough places smooth.'

When they were little, my children had a rock tumbler. They would put rough rocks in and, weeks later, smooth stones would emerge. Rubbing up against each other in the tumbler knocked the jagged edges off the rocks. So it is through the journey of fatherhood.

Graham says that one of the impacts of children is to 'knock off the rough spots', and he acknowledges he has changed through his experience of being a dad. As we walk the path that God has set before us, we make it smoother, but at the same time we are softened ourselves.

Graham trusted his Father in heaven. And now Alfie is trusting all six feet and seven inches of his new dad.

8

Losing-it dad – Paul

A major breakdown, followed by a spiritual rebirth, made this former police officer reconsider his priorities in life and rebuild a relationship with his long-suffering family. So, what lessons can he now share with other men whose lives are spiralling out of control?

'I knew I'd reached the end,' says Paul. 'My thinking was all skewed.'

The retired police constable from Leicester sits before me with piercing blue eyes and shaved grey hair. There's an arm tattoo of a cross poking out from under his polo shirt and a Men United symbol for the charity Prostate Cancer UK on the lapel of the jacket beside him. For a man who previously tried to take his own life, he looks remarkably calm.

'I had decided I didn't want a slow death,' he says matter-of-factly, as if discussing what he was going to have for dinner that night. 'I knew the Swain Street railway bridge in Leicester. It's easy to climb the girders and then back along the wall with the train tracks below. It was perfect.'

Paul decided to jump from the infamous East Midlands bridge on New Year's Eve 1995. He left a Leicester social club, where the crowd was singing 'Auld Lang Syne' at midnight, and walked around in the dark until climbing the bridge around 2.00 am. But he couldn't jump.

'I wasn't even man enough to kill myself,' he remembers. 'Now I know it was the God I didn't want to know intervening when I needed him most.'

Life on Mars

Today, Paul, 56, is Regional Director, England (North) for Christian Vision for Men (cvm.org.uk). He has been married to Sue since 1985 and has two adult daughters, Amy and Hayley, plus four grandchildren.

We meet at the offices of CVM in Chesterfield, where Paul is loading the 'mission motor', as he refers to his car, to take part in a conference in Yorkshire for men, some of whose lives have gone off the rails.

He feels well placed to be included. Back in the mid 1990s, Paul's life didn't so much go off the rails as crash head first into the barrier: there was the drink and experimentation with drugs, running up huge debts to feed his addictions; the affair and then turning his back on his family; the failed suicide bid and subconscious cry for help. He was spiralling downwards.

'We worked hard and played hard in the police. It was,' he laughs, 'just like the TV police series *Life on Mars*. That culture has thankfully long gone. We were generational diehards – men brought up in a culture of tightly defined role models.'

Paul joined the police in 1981, aged 21. He worked closely with another young man, who like Paul was suddenly exposed to the darker side of life at a tender age through the nature of his work. The pair progressed to roles in the Criminal Investigation Department and the caseload increased – as did the severity of the crimes. Then, one late-summer evening in 1995, Paul's colleague took his own life by gassing himself in his car. Paul's life, both professionally and personally, fell apart in a heartbeat.

'I tried to process why he hadn't said anything to me. After all,' says Paul, 'I was his friend. I couldn't cope with the grief but, when I was sent to see the welfare officer, they told me to "pull myself together".'

'So I hit the bottle and started getting into the odd punch-up with colleagues in bars. I was only pain-free when I was asleep, so I started inducing sleep with booze and other substances not currently available over the counter in Boots,' he adds with a touch of the gallows humour you find only with someone who has been to the edge and stared into the abyss.

'I couldn't admit I had a mental-health problem to my employer. I didn't even know that I might have one. I knew the stigma attached to it,' says Paul. 'In that kind of working culture, men just didn't talk about their feelings. That was something only my wife Sue's namby-pamby friends from church would do.'

'Ironically,' he adds 'some of her church friends were actually telling her, "Get rid of him. He's a loser." And I was.'

Paul was diagnosed with severe depression. He turned up at the local vicarage in early January 1996 and asked the vicar to accompany him as he went to tell his wife about the affair and the £10,000 debt. 'I was shaking and he had to hold my hand as we walked up the road,' remembers Paul. 'I was not man enough to do it myself.'

Family reunion

It was only after four months off work, periods of psychotherapy and exploring faith that Paul would start to rebuild his relationship with his family. He started by helping out with the play at the school that his two daughters went to.

'I knew that I needed to restore what I had thrown away, so I volunteered to help with the staging. The girls taught me forgiveness in their own little way that summer,' he says. 'It really hit home to me when I looked at their happy little faces on stage to see their dad sitting there for them.'

'I was so proud in that moment, yet I had never felt it before,' he adds. 'Previously, I guess I didn't want to know them at all. I was there when they were both born but, somehow, I had never felt worthy enough to be responsible to be their dad. By this point, I had missed the years of their childhood.'

He talks about this dark period very candidly, and I can tell the sense of shame, the heartbreak that those precious childhood years can never be recovered. We all hurt our families sometimes and we all carry that pain with us. He flashes those blue eyes towards me, world-weary but still with a glimmer of a twinkle.

'We can even laugh about it now as a family but, at the time, I think I just wasn't ready for the responsibility of being a husband and a father,' he says. 'It was the toxic combination of upbringing, job and bullying culture. It broke me.'

Finding faith

Faith was a major part of Paul's healing process. Sue had prayed for him throughout the wild times, and a spiritual encounter in spring 1996 secured his recovery.

'I had always seen the men at Sue's church, wearing their socks and sandals, as weak and lesser men. But when I went with her to a church social event one night, I experienced a huge internal battle,' he remembers.

'I was aware of another presence, a feeling of pure peace. I realised that I needed to build a relationship with Jesus before I could start rebuilding my own family. So, I began by reading a children's Bible. It was a place to start.'

Paul returned to work eventually, joining the Vice Squad in 1998, where he started to work with cases involving sex offenders. But the toxic work culture continued to cast a shadow over his life and Paul faced ridicule for his new-found faith.

'They called me a fruit bat. I knew they would,' he says. 'One day, I came into work and my team had put a purple cloth and candles out on my desk. They were all making gags about my new-found beliefs.'

Paul just laughed it off, his faith unchallenged. 'I'm so grateful to God for enabling me to see a way forward in life,' he says. 'Come the day I stand before him, I have questions to ask and I will ask them.

'But,' he adds, 'I've come to realise that, sometimes, our Lord doesn't come up with the answers that you want or in a way you expect. Like the best fathers, he knows what's best and his timing is always perfect.'

Talking therapy

Paul finally retired from the police in 2011. These days, he spends a lot of time listening, primarily to men whose lives have fallen apart. He regularly talks to men's groups and conferences as part of his role with CVM.

All the latest research indicates that men are struggling more and more with their gender roles, their work–life balance and their ability to speak up about their inner demons. Male suicide rates are rising rapidly, particularly in young men and those in midlife, yet images of men presented in mainstream media and advertising are often outdated at best or set up for ridicule at worst.

'Men try to solve stuff – it's in their nature,' he says. 'But I believe that many things, such as televised sport and cheap supermarket beer, have stopped us men from talking about our problems. There is no environment for men to naturally get together. It's only when we hit the wall that we realise something is wrong.

'The truth is,' he adds, 'most men are actually quite good at holding it together and not spiralling out of control. But when we do spiral, we completely lose the plot. Nowadays I get emails all the time from men on the edge – just like I was, standing on the railway bridge that night and about to throw myself to my death.'

'The answer is, in many ways, quite simple.' He flashes the baby blues one more time and puts on his jacket. There's work to do, introducing men to their Saviour.

'I just try to get them together with a bunch of fellas to share and talk,' he smiles. 'Men just talking about their feelings. Now there's a concept.'

Dad tips

A dad can be put on a pedestal, but it's important to show that you're a flawed human being too.

Never tell your child that they are stupid or undermine them with other derogatory comments. What they might do may be seen as stupid but that's very different.

The best things in life are not possessions. It's your time that children crave. You cannot buy that.

Hayley says...

'I think it's important to be honest (age appropriate, obviously) as dads and show that you're a flawed human being too. I think that creates a depth of relationship that's more real. Being able to laugh with and at each other is also so important.'

Amy says...

'A dad is the man a girl looks to model her husband on. My dad nurtured me from a little girl and is now someone I love spending time with. He equipped me with the tools to carry me through my grown-up life, and I've now adopted these into my own children's lives.'

Male breakdown facts, UK

- 34%: percentage of men who would be embarrassed or ashamed to take time off work for a mental-health concern, such as anxiety or depression, compared with 13% for a physical injury.
- 38%: percentage of men who would be concerned that their employer would think badly of them if they took time off work for a mental-health concern, compared with 26% for a physical injury.
- 191,000: number of men a year reporting stress, depression or anxiety caused or made worse by work according to a 2016 report for the Health and Safety Executive.
- 12%: proportion of men who said that the last time they were prompted to take time off work to see a GP was because they were 'constantly feeling stressed or under pressure'. Some 11% said it was because of 'prolonged feelings of sadness'.
- Men are nearly 50% more likely than women to be treated compulsorily as psychiatric inpatients.
- Men have measurably lower access to the social support of friends, relatives and the community.
- Men commit 86% of violent crime and are twice as likely to be victims of violent crime as women.

Sources: Men's Health Forum (www.menshealthforum.org.uk); Office for National Statistics (www.ons.gov.uk)

The Samaritans' report

Men, Suicide and Society, a 2012 report by the Samaritans, emphasised that middle-aged men in lower socio-economic groups are at a particularly high risk of suicide.

It pointed to the interaction of complex factors, such as unemployment and economic hardship, a lack of close social and family relationships, the influence of a historical culture of masculinity, personal crises such as divorce, as well as a general 'dip' in subjective well-being among people in their midlife years, compared with both younger and older people.

The report's findings were split into six key themes:

- Personality traits – some traits can interact with factors such as deprivation, unemployment, social disconnection and triggering events, such as relationship breakdown or job loss, to increase the risk of suicide.
- Masculinity – more than women, men respond to stress by taking risks, like misusing alcohol and drugs.
- Relationship breakdowns – marriage breakdown is more likely to lead men, rather than women, to suicide.
- Challenges of midlife – people currently in midlife are experiencing more mental-health problems and unhappiness compared with younger and older people.
- Emotional illiteracy – men are much less likely than women to have a positive view of counselling or therapy, and when they do use these services, it is at the point of crisis.
- Socio-economic factors – unemployed people are two-to-three times more likely to die by suicide than those in work, and suicide increases during economic recession.

Source: www.samaritans.org/sites/default/files/kcfinder/files/Men%20 and%20Suicide%20Research%20Report%20210912.pdf

Reflection

If I asked you to tell me about your football injury, the time you fell off a ladder or the operation you've just had, you could probably wax lyrical about the gruesome details and the lingering after-effects. However, if I invited you to tell me about your mental state and to describe your sadnesses, anxieties, panic attacks, depression, suicidal thoughts or breakdown, I suspect you would be a little more cagey. Why do we feel at ease telling stories of our physical wounds, but keep those of our mental ones hidden? Is it because our minds are closely associated with our characters, so to admit any mental struggles feels like an attack on the core of who we are? Or could it be that we think a physical break heals and normal strength returns, whereas a mental break leaves a lasting weakness – a weakness we are ashamed of?

I'm glad Paul has told his story and allowed us a glimpse into the workings of his mind. In doing so, he has debunked the stigma surrounding mental health and men. He has exploded the myth that men don't need to talk about their feelings. He has shown that there is no shame in weakness.

In 2 Corinthians, the apostle Paul talks about the power of weakness. He says that when he pleaded for God to take away 'a thorn in my flesh, a messenger of Satan' (2 Corinthians 12:7), God said, 'My grace is sufficient for you, for my power is made perfect in weakness' (v. 9). Paul goes on to conclude, 'For when I am weak, then I am strong' (v. 10). When we sincerely accept our own weakness and acknowledge our dependency on God and others, God's grace and power are magnified. Our weakness becomes our strength.

Perhaps when Paul admitted his problems to a vicar, it was the foothold in his heart that God needed to begin renewing him. Paul talks candidly about his new-found dependency when he describes what happened with the vicar: 'I was shaking and he had to hold my hand as we walked up the road,' remembers Paul. 'I was not man enough to do it myself.' After his breakdown, God began to reassemble and restore Paul. A significant effect was that his heart turned back towards his family and he began to re-engage as a father.

When God says, in Malachi 4:6, 'He will turn the hearts of the fathers to their children, and the hearts of the children to their fathers,' he is highlighting the powerful impact of a good relationship between a father, or father figure, and his children. Such a relationship is not only socially important; it is spiritually significant too, and God can use it to heal us and positively influence those around us.

I love it when Paul says, 'I've come to realise that, sometimes, our Lord doesn't come up with the answers that you want or in a way you expect. Like the best fathers, he knows what's best and his timing is always perfect.' 1 Peter 5:7 says, 'Cast all your anxiety on him because he cares for you.' I am reminded that God is the perfect father and wants me to be open when I struggle with worries, dark thoughts and a lack of hope. He is always there, always listening and always caring.

9

Stay-at-home dad – Dave

A life-changing accident led to a role as a pioneering stay-at-home dad. But, as his boys grow and an empty nest looms, what does the future hold for a dedicated dad?

The year was 1981. Dave was a 23-year-old newly qualified geography teacher and had landed a dream job teaching on the subtropical British island territory of Bermuda. Once, after a day in the classroom, he was riding his moped up Burnt House Hill to head into town for a beer. It was raining – hard.

'I remember that I came off my bike and smacked my head. After that,' he says, 'I don't remember a thing. The next thing I knew, I woke up in hospital. The police found my helmet in a bush the next day. The strap wasn't done up properly.'

'I just went back to work after my recovery and carried on,' he adds. 'Initially I didn't even tell my parents. I didn't want to worry them. I remember I just got a road bike instead of my moped.'

He smiles. 'It was fine, just a lot harder work with the heat and humidity of Bermuda.'

Today, Dave is a 58-year-old father to three boys – Jack, 14, and 11-year-old twins Sam and Joe. We're talking over mugs of tea at the kitchen table. The tableware suggests a certain fondness for a Mancunian football team who play in red. The scrawl of black marker pen on the weekly planner on the wall indicates a packed schedule of after-school activities. A magnet on the fridge says, 'Let your light shine through.'

Dave looks fit and wiry for a man in his 50s, with close-cropped grey hair and sparkling eyes. Clad in a green T-shirt and shorts, his bare feet on the terracotta tiles of the kitchen floor, he has the air of a man who makes keeping fit a key part of his daily routine. It's only when he speaks that hints emerge of the story that brought him to this point today.

Back in training

Dave started running and cycling to get his fitness back after the accident. He was soon entering road races and triathlons – until one day he blacked out in the bathroom of his apartment. Not long after he had blackouts in several of his road races.

But, with his newly diagnosed epilepsy controlled by medication, he was soon back competing. He continued with his running and cycling even when he moved back to the UK in 1989. After various teaching roles and time cycling around Australia and New Zealand, he found a job at a school near Wrexham, North Wales.

'It was the last day of term and I was helping to supervise the school disco,' remembers Dave. 'By this time, I hadn't had a seizure for years and I wanted to come off the drugs, so I had started to phase out two of the three pills. I still wouldn't accept they were necessary.'

'Apparently,' he says, 'I had a grand mal seizure at the entrance of the school that afternoon. A few months later I had another while on my bike. I remember I was going to deliver my Father's Day present to my dad.'

'That one,' he adds, 'put me in hospital with broken ribs and smashed-up teeth from smacking my head against the handlebars.'

Family life

Dave met his wife, Lynn, a teacher, when he was leading walking groups for a travel company in school holidays. The following year Dave suffered a series of devastating seizures, which following a long stay in hospital seriously aggravated the brain injury from his previous moped accident. This forced him to take ill-health retirement from teaching.

Dave married Lynn in 2001. Both wanted a family but realised that, given the gravity of Dave's condition, family life would not be straightforward.

'There was a possibility that, given the medication I was on, having children would not be easy. We also decided,' he adds, 'that if we did have kids, then I would stay home and keep house.'

Jack was born in February 2003; the twins followed in May 2005. A stay-at-home dad (SAHD) was virtually unheard of at the time.

'I don't see why a bloke can't look after the kids – if you've got the time. There's nothing a woman can do that a man can't. There was no problem with doing nappies and the feeding. I simply don't consider children to be a woman's job,' says Dave of his early days in the role.

But Dave does rue the way the image of the Fairy Liquid mother from the classic advertisements is still engrained in our collective consciousness as a society, an image further reinforced in films and television.

Dave was reluctant at first to take Jack to the local toddler groups as he was put off by the reactions of the mothers around him. 'It was 2003 and I was the only bloke in the room,' he says. 'It felt a bit awkward but I just got on with it.'

'But when Sam and Joe came along in 2005,' he adds, 'I took all three, with Jack on the Buggy Board. By then, everyone knew us. Some of my happiest memories are trips to the zoo with the three boys. By the time we got to school, people were really nice to us, although I knew many more mums than dads.'

Even today, while society has evolved, some attitudes towards traditional gender roles are still slow to change. 'I was on dinner duty recently at the local school where I work at lunchtimes,' he says. 'A teaching assistant, a nice older lady, didn't bat an eyelid as she said, "Listen to the dinner lady." She never even thought to use the words "midday assistant". People forget the world has moved on.'

Positive outlook

These days Dave is well used to the routine of home life, revolving as it inevitably does around the activities of the three boys. But he also has darker moments.

'It's wonderful to be so closely bonded with the boys as the primary carer at home,' he says. 'But sometimes when I go out I don't have a lot to talk about – apart from the boys. It upsets me that people will put me on the fringe of the conversation just because I don't have a nine-to-five job.'

Society, Dave feels, tends to define us through our jobs. 'When I say that I'm at home, some people think I'm just lazing around all day drinking tea,' he says. 'I just get on with it but it does frustrate me. For example, I was up at 6.30 am this morning and I'll be full belt all day until 9.00 pm this evening.'

Overall, however, Dave retains a remarkably positive outlook on life, and faith is a part of this glass-half-full mentality. He started going to his local Who Let The Dads Out? group with the three boys and did the Daddy Cool course with a community of other local dads.

'Jack has grown up with good morals and attends a youth club linked to the local church. I know what's right and wrong but,' he laughs, 'the boys can quote more passages from the Bible than me.'

This faith also underpins his philosophical approach to life, creating the impression of a man at peace with his lot. Dave's last seizure was in 2008 but he knows his epilepsy is not going away.

'I was always of the mindset that I could do anything. The accident just happened; I'm not bitter,' he says. 'But the way people react does upset me sometimes.'

'They can't see any problem, so people don't understand why I get tired. I can go off at tangents and I forget things easily. They seem frustrated,' he adds, 'but they don't realise there's a lot going on inside the brain.'

Dark days

Dave has enjoyed long years of close bonds with his three boys. More recently, however, Jack has grown into a teenager and the family dynamic has shifted. It's Dave who feels this most keenly.

'I can live with the comments other people make about me being at home, but Jack is now also starting to make comments. That makes me feel this small,' he gestures with his two fingers. 'He thinks I'm useless these days.'

'Of course, it worries me how my relationship with Jack has changed,' he admits. 'Lynn is always telling me off and saying to praise him more, but I seem to have lost him somehow. There are still bonding moments, like being out on a bike ride, but he needs his privacy now.'

'I hope,' he adds, a sadness about his clear green eyes, 'it's just a phase.'

After talking for a while, Dave shows me around the house. The drum kit, set up in the extension, is waiting for someone to bash its skins, and a half-emptied washing basket sits patiently on the kitchen floor, awaiting Dave's attention. A shelf of CDs at the back of the kitchen includes Roxy Music and Paul Weller while the kitchen radio is tuned to Ken Bruce's Popmaster quiz.

In the lounge, a set of three watercolours depicting the boys playing football and running around are proudly hung on the wall. Dave painted them himself at a local art group he joined to keep the grey matter ticking over. 'I find it very therapeutic,' he says, showing his latest work-in-progress, a sketch of a close-up of the smiling faces of the three boys.

'I think we've both been completely committed to the boys as parents and I've been here for them all the time since they were born. At times, of course, it has put pressure on our own relationship,' he says.

'But when we arrive at the empty-nest stage, I fear it will come as a real shock,' he adds. 'I'm trying not to think about it. I mean, I love the walking and the painting but how will I fill the day?'

Overall, Dave plays down the idea he was blazing a trail for other SAHDs to follow. He's quietly philosophical about his lot. 'I was very lucky to have that closeness to the boys at an early age. The question is how to keep that closeness as they grow up and leave home,' he ponders.

'I don't know yet what I can offer them later on.' He smiles. 'But I'll think about it when it comes.'

Dad tips

Talk to your kids and engage with them. You have to keep talking to them.

It's easy to shout sometimes. But try to take a breath and hold back. It's an easy way to make those around you feel isolated.

We always rushed everywhere but, looking back, I'd say to slow down sometimes and appreciate the things around you.

Stay-at-home dad (SAHD) facts

- Reports in the popular media suggest there are some 250,000 SAHDs in the UK.
- However, the Office for National Statistics (ONS) does not collect figures in relation to stay-at-home parents. This means there is no official definition for this role. The National At-Home Dad Network US defines SAHD as 'a father who is the daily, primary caregiver of his children under age 18'.
- According to 'Economic inactivity by reason: looking after family and home' (ONS, 2015), the number of men in this category aged 16–64 between March and May 2015 was 246,000. For women, the figure was 2,020,000.
- The comparable figures for 2013 were 210,000 men versus 2,904,000 women.
- The Modern Fatherhood website states: 'Between 2001 and 2011 the proportion of fathers working 48 or more hours per week has fallen from 40% to 31%, compared with 35% to 29% for all men.'
- According to the most accurate count, by Beth Latshaw of Appalachian State University in 2009, there are 1.4 million SAHDs in the USA. In her study, Latshaw focuses on the role of the father, not their employment status.
- The Pew Research Centre reported in 2014 that the number of SAHDs in the USA had doubled since 1989 to around 2 million.

Sources: dadbloguk.com; National At-Home Dad Network US (athomedad. org); www.ons.gov.uk; www.modernfatherhood.org

Reflection

What defines a man? Is it the loftiness of his position, the size of his pay packet, the trophies in his cabinet? Or is he defined by his willingness to do the unnoticed and shun the accolades, to make sacrifices and go out on a limb?

Dave's fridge magnet says, 'Let your light shine through,' probably a reference to Matthew 5:16: 'Let your light shine before others, that they may see your good deeds and glorify your Father in heaven.'

What kind of light shines through Dave's story? For me, it is courage.

Which is the more courageous way? Is it to choose your challenges, calculate the risks, make your plans and give it a try? Or is it to take the blows from the unexpected slings and arrows of life with a resolute determination to keep going in whatever way you can?

Dave's courage is the quiet, unassuming kind. He has the heart of a lion, but expresses himself with the tenderness of a lamb. He is a world traveller, an adventurer and a sportsman, but he is also a loyal family man, a loving husband and a thoughtful father. Dave swam against the tide of popular opinion about the right role for a father, and he became a stay-at-home dad with few peers. 'I was the only bloke in the room,' he says '... but I just got on with it.' That's courage.

When men come to tell Jairus that his daughter has died and for him not to bother Jesus any more, Jesus reassures Jairus by saying, 'Don't be afraid; just believe' (Mark 5:36). Dave did just believe: he believed that looking after children was as much a role for a father as a mother; he believed that he could do the job; and he believed that it was the right thing for his family that he become a stay-at-home dad.

The bit when he talks about his changing relationship with Jack touches me most, and I believe that it is because Dave has been such a good father that Jack is questioning him. Jack is beginning to navigate a route to manhood, emerging from his father's shadow to become his own man, and he feels safe to test his thinking with Dave. He is expressing opinions to see how they fit, like trying on shoes. Sometimes we try on shoes knowing they are unsuitable, but we give them a go anyway just to see how they feel.

We often do the same with God, our heavenly Father. We doubt his existence, we question his motives and we forget what he has done for us. God takes it on the chin, and at the end of it all we can often find ourselves closer to him than ever before. Some things remain a mystery, but our faith in him can become stronger because of our struggles to understand him.

Dave hopes that Jack's dissent will be a phase, and I'm sure it will be. Within another decade Jack will be a man who sees his father's courage and recognises that his dad never gave up. He fought adversity with a nappy bag and a buggy, and like God he gave his children a rare but special model of fatherhood.

10

Searching dad – Richard

The loss of a father figure in early childhood left a gaping void and split a family apart. But what does the experience of one young man in the 1950s teach us about the state of modern fatherhood today?

Richard has just one memory of his father – and he treasures it.

He was 4 years old and living in Maidstone, Kent, when his father – then serving in World War II – came home on leave.

'We were eating Sunday lunch at home,' remembers Richard. 'Halfway through I went and sat on dad's lap. My mum told me to get down but he said, "If he's going to grow into a man, then he needs to eat a man's meal."'

'This is,' he says, visibly moved by the memory, 'the only time I had with him and I knew he loved me.'

The soldier died in action in 1944 and Richard's life would soon spin out of control. Over 70 years later, he feels he is still coming to terms with it.

Family drama

Richard doesn't look the sentimental sort. Indeed, the first things I notice when we meet at a station cafe in the commuter belt of Crawley are the strong, weathered hands and bushy eyebrows. Richard may be 77 years old but he looks strong, a testament to the years working outdoors as a gardener. It's only the heavy-set eyes that betray the sadness that has stayed with him since his early childhood.

'I still have the feeling I was unloved as a child. I just wish my mother had cuddled me more,' says Richard. Customers grab takeaway coffees and dash for trains around us while he starts to open up his heart to me.

'It has taken me an exceptionally long time and a lot of God's guidance to heal. Maybe, at my age, I can finally reflect and see things with more perspective. I feel,' he adds pensively, 'that I can now talk about it.'

After his father's death, the family struggled to cope with the loss and the young Richard looked to his two elder brothers, Bob and especially David, who was six years older, as father figures. By the time he was 14, Richard's mother had developed cancer and was confined to a nursing home, where she died. Richard left school soon afterwards and the brothers drifted apart.

'I always longed for my eldest brother, David, to take more interest in me. I watched him grow to become the man I wanted to be my father. He was my hero and I wanted to be just like him,' says Richard.

'Looking back,' he adds, 'I was living in a fantasy world from the ages of 4 to 10. I was different, probably difficult, and a real loner. I lied. I told stories all the time. But I just wanted a father and a home. The point is this: we all need a father figure in life.'

With the family torn apart, Richard's uncle helped to arrange an assisted passage to Australia for five pounds. Richard left England in February 1956 and docked in Fremantle one month later – the day of his 16th birthday. He ended up taking a job on a farm in the Hunter Valley, located north of Sydney in New South Wales, and spent five years working the land on farms around eastern Australia. He struggled to make friends and develop close relationships. He tells me that he often felt very alone, especially as all communication with his eldest brother ceased.

I can't help but feel sympathy for Richard as we talk over the clatter of the coffee cups. As an only child, I remember the sense of loss of a playmate when my grandfather died. I was 10. But Richard spent much of his childhood alone, the people he was desperate to connect with turning their backs on him. It's an experience that has clearly scarred him for life. Indeed, his only source of comfort during this time abroad was what he describes as a 'spiritual experience'.

'I was milking the cows one day on the farm, singing hymns in the dairy, particularly "Oh come to my heart, Lord Jesus, there is room in my heart for thee"', he remembers. 'I leaned against a cow and felt its warmth. Then I started crying hysterically. I felt at that moment that Jesus was with me.'

'I feel I have made peace with life now, although there are still some issues,' he says. 'Ever since that day, whenever I have shared my feelings with God, he has accepted me and helped me to find another perspective.'

'It has been,' he finally sighs, a burden of pain perhaps lifting as we speak, 'a journey of healing ever since.'

Prodigal return

Richard returned to the UK in August 1960, taking a series of jobs in Yorkshire at first. There wasn't much stability to his life and he drifted through years of small jobs and rented rooms.

'Sometimes I was running away. Sometimes I felt I was being pushed away. But I always felt I was being rejected somehow. I just wasn't good enough for anyone,' he says.

Eventually he settled down and married in 1969, fathering two daughters, but the marriage failed and Richard found himself alone with the two girls after his wife left. He was desperate to reconnect with his brothers, but there was no communication. It was only when he met his current wife, Angela, that he formed a more stable, blended family. His girls were aged 9 and 6; her son and daughter were 7 and 5. Some 30 years later, they remain a strong family group and committed to God.

'Despite the lack of a father figure in my own life, I tried to be a good father to my two daughters and, subsequently, to another son and daughter from my second marriage,' says Richard. 'I got a lot wrong. I didn't give them any spiritual training or instil any standards but, at least, I was there for them and I loved them.'

Family reunion

Richard was baptised in 1986 and embarked upon a process of prayer, counselling and healing. He subsequently started to pray for reconciliation between himself and his brothers and, in 1999, met up with David for the first time in 47 years. The rendezvous was set at a car park in Crawley.

'I was very excited to see my brother again that day but, when I arrived, he wouldn't get out of his van. So I sat there with him and his wife in the back seat. He was clearly very uncomfortable with the situation,' remembers Richard.

David later held a party for his golden wedding anniversary and invited both brothers, and their wives, to attend.

'As we sat down for lunch, it occurred to me that it was exactly 50 years since they had dropped me at Liverpool Street station to head to the ship for Australia,' says Richard.

During that time, he had seen David just once, while contact with the second brother, Bob, was occasional at best. 'I still felt a sense of love for them but couldn't show that to them outwardly that day. I didn't think they were ready for that,' he says.

It was Bob who called in March 2016 to say that David had died.

'I felt a sense of release,' says Richard. 'I could finally talk about my life story without upsetting him. But it was amazing just how many people at David's funeral came up to me and said, "We never knew David had another brother."'

Paternal figure

Richard believes his experience of life has taught him about the importance of male role models – for security, mental well-being and emotional attachment.

'A major part of the pain in family life today is the rejection by fathers of their sons,' he says. 'Maybe my story will help people understand the pain of that rejection. I know that I've struggled with it all my life. The standards a father sets are the standards a boy will live by. A boy going through puberty has no idea how to become a man. Boys who are rejected are more likely to bottle it up and struggle to manage it.'

Richard looks thoughtful. The constant stream of commuters is buzzing around the cafe like flies, the coffee machine is spluttering and wheezing like an old asthmatic. But Richard is oblivious, lost in his thoughts. He is passionate about the tough life lessons he has learned first-hand.

As I sit there, he makes me think about what life lessons my own father taught me and assess the examples in life I set to my daughters. We all need role models in life but, knowing now the pressures fatherhood can put you under, I can understand better the times my own father seemed distant or distracted. Ultimately, we're all just doing our best.

'The importance of dads is not being talked up. That's wrong. We should be shouting from the rooftops,' he says.

'But I can't bridge the divide on my own,' he adds. 'I would like to feel that men now are accepted and acceptable. They seem to understand better the value of relationships. As men start to take responsibility for who they are and what they are, they start to understand how valuable they really are.'

Looking back

Richard has the benefit of hindsight that comes with age. I can sense his innate wisdom – even above the train announcements. As he enters his late 70s and his role as a father and grandfather evolves, he can see in context how those formative experiences shaped his whole outlook on life. That's why he founded Time Out for Dads, an organisation for fathers similar to Who Let The Dads Out?, for men in and around Crawley.

'I know one day I'm going to die but I feel more at peace with that now than ever before,' he says. 'I have less fear of being rejected. That's not saying the anxiety has completely gone but I'm confident that God will accept me.'

'What I've learned,' he adds, 'is that men need to seek out and learn what it means to be a man. To really hit it home, how to be a father and husband should be taught in schools.'

And when the day comes to meet his maker? Richard smiles. 'When I see my dad one day in heaven,' he says, 'I'll say to him, "Dad, it's lovely to see you again."'

Dad tip

You just have to love your children. Don't condemn. Just let them know they are accepted.

Father-figure facts

- £48 billion: the cost of family breakdown to UK taxpayers in 2016, an increase for the seventh year in a row from £37 billion in 2009
- 50%: the chance that children will still be living with both birth parents by the time they are 16
- £1,820 per annum: the financial burden on the average UK taxpayer of family breakdowns in 2016, a rise of £274 from the previous year
- 83%: proportion of 2,000 adults in a 2011 poll who thought family breakdown was a serious problem; over a third thought it was very serious
- 75%: proportion of 2,000 adults in a 2011 poll who thought fatherlessness was a serious problem; almost a third thought it was very serious
- 63%: proportion of youth suicides from fatherless homes
- 90%: proportion of homeless and runaway children from fatherless homes
- 85%: proportion of children who show behaviour disorders from fatherless homes
- 25%: the amount by which a boy's chances of escaping poverty are reduced if his father has low interest in his education
- 70% (two-parent-family fathers) and 81% (non-resident parents, mainly men): percentage of fathers wanting to be more involved in their children's education but feeling exasperated by school processes and attitudes that fail to include non-resident fathers
- 80%: percentage of children excluded from school in years 10 and 11 that have problems traced back to poor literacy levels in years 3 and 4. Numerous studies demonstrate that language exposure in early life has a significant effect on later verbal skills
- 400,000: number of families headed by lone fathers in 2012, representing 13.5% of all single-parent households in the UK. With an average number of children per family of 2.32, there were 928,000 children in lone-father families in the UK in 2012

Sources: www.relationshipsfoundation.org; www.centreforsocialjustice. org.uk; www.fatherhoodinstitute.org; Office for National Statistics (www. ons.gov.uk); www.fatherfigure.org.uk; US Department of Health/Census, 2011

Reflection

Who do you belong to? I am not asking about ownership – whose property you are – but about where you feel at home, attached and accepted. You may be a member of a club or a society, a church or a political party, a workplace or a group of friends. But many, perhaps most, would say that first and foremost they belong to their families, and their families are the anchoring point that gives them the security to venture through life.

In *Meeting God at Every Turn*, Catherine Marshall writes:

> The family is meant to be the training ground for life, a true microcosm of the world outside the home where person has to get along with person, pupils with each other and with teachers, employees with bosses, management with labor, nation with nation.

But what if you don't have that training ground – if the family you are a part of disintegrates? Where does your preparation for life come from then?

Richard has had a hole in his life, and it is a burden he has always had to bear. He yearned for a sense of belonging to his family and hungered for a father who loved him and accepted him. As a consequence of their absence he was unprepared for life and he struggled to develop friendships and deepen relationships, being scared of rejection and often feeling alone.

Even those whose fathers are alive can feel abandoned, because their fathers are either physically absent or emotionally distant. Richard says that the only time he felt his father loved him was when his dad allowed him to sit on his lap at the table even though his mother had told him to get down. It reminds me of the time when Jesus admonished his disciples for trying to stop the little children coming to him (Matthew 19:13–14). Jesus accepted the children and encouraged them; by his words and actions he let them know how valuable they were. In that unique moment during Sunday lunch, Richard got a small glimpse of his father's love. Did it make him feel the same as those small children crowding around Jesus?

Like Richard, it may be difficult to feel valuable if your father has left you, even if he did not do so voluntarily. Richard has found acceptance and a place of belonging with his heavenly Father. I guess it will not have been easy because how do you relate to a spiritual father when you have no experience of relating to an earthly one? But God is patient, and he is gentle. Richard's 'journey of healing' has been a long one and he now feels some peace because he is confident that God will accept him. The Bible tells us that God does indeed accept Richard, because he is a child of God: 'See what great love the Father has lavished on us, that we should be called children of God! And that is what we are!' (1 John 3:1).

Richard felt unloved as a child, but he has since discovered that he is loved by a Father who is always there, always welcoming and always dependable, a Father to whom we can all belong.

Afterword

Eighty years, then, of Father's Day.

The whole way we think about fathers has changed – from the distant Victorian dad to the hands-on, multitasking, nappy-changing, work–life-juggling dad of today. Our role as men has changed, too, from hunter-gatherers to nurturing bedrocks of emotional support. Yet men are often ridiculed in adverts as hapless, and they often struggle to understand how their role in society has changed.

As I write the closing lines of this book, the InsideMAN website (www.inside-man.co.uk) is highlighting through its social media channels how the television comedy chat show *All Round to Mrs Brown's* has triggered outrage among domestic-violence campaigners after it passed off the domestic abuse of a man as comedy. The true story, recounted to the man-in-drag presenter by the daughter, a guest on the programme, about her family life as a child, was of a particularly violent episode. 'There's still a dent in the wall from where she threw a knife at him – he says it's a constant reminder to stay on her good side,' the woman said of her parents' relationship, to uproarious laugher from the studio audience.

Reality check: some 450,000 men per year are victims of partner abuse and one in every six men will suffer abuse in their lifetime, according to the Office for National Statistics.

Mark Brooks, chairman of the ManKind Initiative, a national charity supporting male victims of domestic abuse, subsequently called for an apology from the BBC. He told InsideMAN: 'It is frankly staggering this was ever broadcast by the BBC let alone treated as funny and a cause for celebration.'

Golden age

At a time of fundamental change, then, is masculinity, and by extension fatherhood, locked into a moment of crisis?

'No,' says Mark Chester, founder of Who Let The Dads Out? 'I believe we are living in a golden age of fatherhood. Fathers are expected, and given permission, to get involved with the lives of their kids more than ever. It's a great opportunity for men to seize that moment and be a bigger part of their lives.'

'But,' he adds, 'they face an identity crisis. Men were traditionally both the breadwinner and the light relief at the end of the day but, as that role has changed, they must seize the opportunity to change their identity as fathers within society.'

Rob Parsons, author of the seminal book *The Sixty Minute Father*, also recognises the contradiction at the heart of modern fatherhood. 'All the surveys show fathers spend more time with their children. They are more involved with them. Yet our working lives are more intense and fragile,' he tells me over coffee in a Manchester hotel lobby before a speaking engagement that evening.

'So the modern dad has a dilemma: we are there for our children physically but often not there mentally,' he explains. 'We are the first generation with nowhere to hide while put under pressure to do more with our kids.'

'The idea that fatherhood is somehow easier or harder than before is a nonsense,' he smiles. 'It's just that the pressures are different.'

His almond-coloured eyes sparkle behind wire-framed spectacles. 'It may have been easier in that the roles were more clearly defined in the past, but it was certainly less fulfilling,' he adds.

Next generation

Given that the rules have changed, then, what legacy of lessons can we bequeath to the next 80 years of fathers?

For Mark Chester, it's about following our instincts. 'I suspect that, at heart, fathers always wanted to be involved in the lives of their children. So maybe we need to be less swayed by the societal pressures around us. Plus, there's a responsibility on us all to do more community-centred fathering, not just be responsible for our own kids,' he says.

'After all,' he adds, 'we have a natural instinct to take care of our own. So, we should see this as an age of opportunity.'

Rob Parsons offers a pragmatic vision when he takes to the stage to share his own experiences as a father and a grandfather that evening. This chief executive of the charity Care for the Family talks about the 'stiff upper lip of fatherhood', recounting how his own father, 'a grumpy, uncommunicative man' brought stability and presence to the home. 'He would always say, "A mother for love. A father for discipline",' Rob tells the crowd.

Despite the elaborate stage show with its living-room set up and moody lighting, I catch a glimpse of the humble, thoughtful man I met earlier that day, scribbling little biro notes on the back of his olive-skinned hands in the hotel lobby.

His message is carpe diem. 'The role of fathers, and mothers, will continue to be crucial in the future. But, increasingly, our kids will judge us by a single statement: "Were they there for me?" So, make the most of your time together. Grasp the moment,' he says. 'The mistake we all make is to think, "One day we will have more time together"'.

Personal experience

As for me? Well, meeting the ten fathers whose stories cry out from the pages of this book has left me with a vision of the future whereby fathers will continue to overcome life's slings and arrows to love their children. Their bravery, dedication and honesty are truly an inspiration.

I've also seen how, no matter what has gone before, it's never too late to learn, to do our best to be better men and better dads. But I've also learned that sometimes we should cut ourselves some slack – step back, take stock and maybe even venture a manly pat on the back. No, really.

I've been trying hard for over ten years now and, entering my 46th year to heaven, I still am. I believe I have, at times, been a good dad. The bedtime stories, the back-breaking hours hunched over bikes, teaching my daughters to cycle in the local park. These were moments I was present in body and mind. But, of course, my parenting skills have been severely lacking at times, especially when stress or tiredness got the better of me. The fact I was doing much of it on my own at times has naturally coloured my experience. I'm no expert, no role model, no visionary.

I'm just doing my best. And if I can offer one top tip for the next 80 years, then it is as simple as that: do your best.

From Prince William to Rob Parsons via the ten good men and true whose collected ordinary stories are extraordinary in many ways, we're all just doing our best.

Why? Because dads care too.

Appendix: 80 dad tips

Each of the interviewees offered their own top dad tips as part of their story. We would like to use these to begin a list, aiming for 80 dad tips to celebrate 80 years of Father's Day.

So please join the conversation by sharing your tips via Twitter and other social media platforms, using the hashtag #80DadTips. Your tips will pass on wisdom to the next 80 years of fathers.

1. Be the superhero. Our children offer unconditional love so being a superhero to our children simply means showing them love, compassion and attention.
2. Never promise what you can't keep. When we break promises, we make lost generations.
3. Talk to your kids and engage with them. You have to keep talking to them.
4. It's easy to shout sometimes. But try to take a breath and hold back. It's an easy way to make those around you feel isolated.
5. We always rushed everywhere but, looking back, I'd say to slow down sometimes and appreciate the things around you.
6. Being a stepfather is about being the dose of reality. You have to be prepared to put in the graft.
7. A stepfather role gives you a good perspective and room to stand back, balancing being responsible with a sense of separation. I feel like I'm 80% stepfather and 20% friend.
8. Don't focus on your own grief and loss.
9. Try not to become isolated.
10. Try to establish new networks in new environments with new people.
11. Be available for your children. I always remember that when my dad was home, he was home.

12 A dad can be put on a pedestal, but it's important to show that you're a flawed human being too.

13 Never tell your child that they are stupid or undermine them with other derogatory comments. What they might do may be seen as stupid but that's very different..

14 The best things in life are not possessions. It's your time that children crave. You cannot buy that.

15 You just have to love your children. Don't condemn. Just let them know they are accepted.

16 Make the most of the time you have with your children. Once it's gone, it's gone.

17 Don't let the hurts of your childhood affect your relationship with your kids. Do all that you can to make peace with your past.

18 Build up a network of supportive friends – other dads that can be there for you (and you for them).

19 Communication: be honest and open about what you're feeling while you're apart.

20 When you're home and with the family, give them your undivided time.

21 You've got to fit in with their routines and what they're doing.

22 Play together. Make time to play something with your little one, even if it's only a short game. It's stress relief for you, and builds skills in your child beyond what you can see.

23 Share your problems. Too many parents try to 'be strong' in front of their children. Share with them your problems (within reason), discuss solutions and share how you worked through solving the problem.

24 Be an example rather than point to one. Actions really do speak louder than words.

25 Over to you…

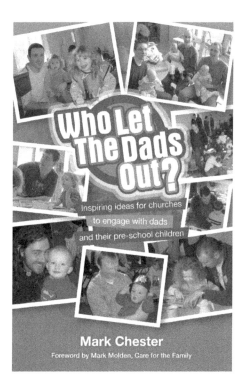

Parent and toddler work can transform relationships and strengthen families, yet sometimes men may have very limited access to the parent and toddler world. This book tells the story of how Who Let The Dads Out? came into being. It gives a practical guide for setting up and running the monthly sessions, complete with theological background, real-life case studies, helpful hints and tips, and twelve easy craft ideas.

Who Let The Dads Out?
Inspiring ideas for churches to engage with dads and their pre-school children
Mark Chester
978 0 84101 885 0 £6.99

brfonline.org.uk

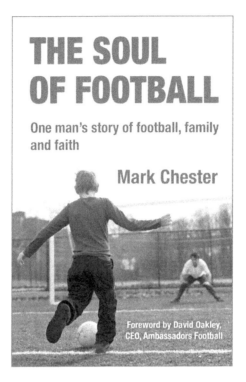

THE SOUL OF FOOTBALL

One man's story of football, family and faith

Mark Chester

Foreword by David Oakley, CEO, Ambassadors Football

In *The Soul of Football*, Mark Chester looks back at his early dreams and aspirations and considers, through the events of his own life and reflections such as 'Understanding the coach' and 'Playing by the rules', what life lessons the 'beautiful game' has taught him.

The Soul of Football
One man's story of football, family and faith
Mark Chester
978 1 84101 654 2 £6.99

brfonline.org.uk

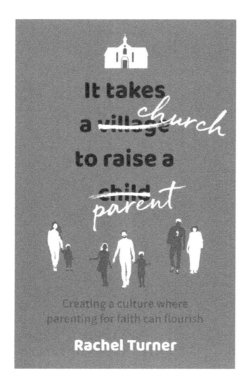

Parents are the primary disciplers of their children, but we as a church are called to be their community who supports them as a family, equips them to succeed, and cheers them on the path of parenting for faith. This book will help children's, youth and senior leaders to learn how to position themselves for maximum impact, develop foundational values and practices to operate out of, and establish practical steps to shape a culture where parenting for faith can flourish.

It Takes a Church to Raise a Parent
Creating a culture where parenting for faith can flourish
Rachel Turner
978 0 85746 625 9 £8.99

brfonline.org.uk

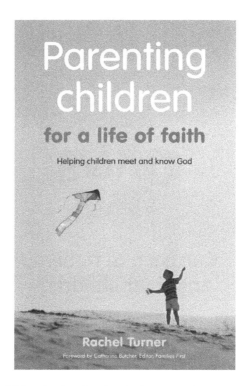

Nurturing children in the Christian faith is a privilege given to all of us whose prime job it is to raise children. God's desire is that our parenting should guide each child to meet and know him, and to live with him every day through to eternity. *Parenting Children for a Life of Faith* explores how the home can become the primary place in which children are nurtured into the reality of God's presence and love, equipped to access him themselves and encouraged to grow In a two-way relatlonshlp wlth hlm that will last a lifetime.

Parenting Children for a Life of Faith
Helping children meet and know God
Rachel Turner
978 1 84101 607 8 £7.99

brfonline.org.uk

Outreach to fathers and their children

Relatively few churches intentionally focus on reaching out to fathers, father figures and their children. BRF's Who Let The Dads Out? programme is working to challenge, inspire and support churches to develop their ministry in this area.

Find out more at **wholetthedadsout.org.uk**